AEC TRUCKS IN CAMERA

S.W. STEVENS~STRATTEN

LONDON

IAN ALLAN LTD

First published 1984
Reprinted 1996

ISBN 0 7110 1443 4

Published by Ian Allan Ltd, Shepperton, Surrey;
and printed by Ian Allan Printing Ltd,
Coombelands House, Addlestone, Surrey KT15 1HY

Publisher's Note
Readers will appreciate that this book was first
published a number of years ago and that, in a
number of cases, the reproduction of certain
illustrations is not of the quality that can be
achieved using modern methods of production.

Contents

Introduction

Originally set up as a bus maintenance and building concern, the Associated Equipment Company entered the field of commercial vehicle production as a result of a wartime contract for the supply of army lorries in 1914.

Becoming part of the London Underground Group of companies supplying 'General' — and later London Transport — with their buses, it was not long before they adopted the slogan 'Builders of London's Buses'. Many technical and design innovations were instigated on the passenger vehicle side and it appeared that commercial vehicles often took second place. The fortunes of the company fell on hard times in the mid-1920s, with competitors updating their designs and thus gaining sales, while the AEC models were looking rather dated. Overtures were made to Leyland Motors regarding the

merger but, fortunately, this never materialised at the time as AEC then started a slow but steady upward trend.

A move to a new and purpose built factory at Southall in 1927 enabled the company to increase production and with new and revolutionary designs from the brain of their new engineer and designer, John G. Rackham, the company really found its feet. In the 1930s they soon made strong inroads into the commercial vehicle market, becoming one of the foremost manufacturers of the heavier type of goods vehicle. The sales figures show how popular the marque became and many well known hauliers and road transport operators relied on the Southall products for their entire fleet.

The company had made a marketing agreement with the Daimler concern in 1926, but this proved unsatisfactory and only lasted a couple of years. The

ompany then remained aloof from any association with other companies, apart from taking over the British section of Four Wheel Drive (FWD) and its renamed successor Hardy Rail Motors, for over 20 years.

With an enviable wartime production record, AEC soon got back to civilian production after hostilities ceased and in 1948 took control of both the Maudslay Motor Co and Crossley Motors, shortly afterwards changing their official name to Associated Commercial Vehicles Ltd. A year later they took over the body building firms of Park Royal Vehicles and its subsidiary Charles H. Roe of Leeds, although apart from the production of cabs this had little effect on commercial vehicle production.

The AEC vehicles were still 'conservative' in their appearance and design and externally they looked little different from their models of 20 years earlier, until the adoption of the 'rounded cabs' in 1955. However, over the years they had undertaken much development work on the diesel engine, culminating in powerful, quiet and smooth running units. Much of the success of AEC can be attributed to their original design of both chassis and components and the large measure of standardisation of parts spread over their range of models.

In 1957 AEC entered the then expanding business of earth moving equipment by producing large dumptrucks. Their last acquisition was in 1961 when they absorbed the old established firm of Thornycroft (Transport Equipment Ltd) into the AEC empire.

A year later AEC was in financial trouble and after secret negotiations with both the British Motor Corporation (Austin and Morris) and Rolls-Royce, it was announced that AEC were to merge with their old rivals, Leyland Motors who had turned down such a proposal 34 years earlier. Whether the capital investment in acquiring Thornycroft proved too much is debatable but it must be remembered that at this time there was a rapid decline in the bus industry, mainly due to an increasing majority of the population owning their own cars, plus the fact that the long relationship with London Transport, as a sole supplier of buses, was coming to an end, thus a steady market was drying up.

The commercial vehicle side should have been able to stand on its own feet, but possibly the AEC models were again becoming dated and being surpassed by other manufacturers in the market. Many people were of the opinion that the announcement of the marger spelt the extinction of AEC, and certainly there was much duplication of models in their respective ranges, yet Leyland permitted the AEC range to continue much longer than AEC kept both the Maudslay or Thornycroft ranges!

Although it could not be foreseen at the time of the merger, the Leyland Motor Corporation, as it had become in 1968, were more or less forced by the government to take control of the ailing British Motor Corporation who were mass producing motor cars and light vans, but who also owned Guy Motors and the Daimler Company. Thus there was even more duplication on an even bigger scale, but equally disastrous was the need for money to be pumped into the car production

which should have been allocated for commercial vehicle development. It must also be borne in mind that at the same time Great Britain was entering the European Economic Community (better than as the Common Market) and the great influx of foreign vehicles at competitive prices seriously affected further sales.

Some pieces of bad luck, misfortune, and/or sheer stupidity and mismanagement by the joint AEC/Leyland control virtually closed the export market. The AEC joint venture with the French organisation Willeme, begun in 1958 whereby AECs with a French cab were being built, was terminated in favour of the new Leyland agreement with Hotchkiss. However the latter never materialised and the Willeme one had already been shut-off. A somewhat similar case occurred with the Netherlands; while the South American and South African markets more or less closed due to restrictions on imports while other countries found the continental manufacturers were able to sustain a better supply of new vehicles together with adequate parts and after sales service.

In 1969 AEC tried to make a come-back with the new V8 engine and optional semi-automatic transmission. Unfortunately, due to lack of finance the engine had not been sufficiently developed and tested and it failed miserably which severely tarnished the old AEC reputation for reliability

Slowly the AEC range was withdrawn and ceased in 1973, although buses continued for a further 18 months. It is significant that the last vehicle to leave the Southall factory when it closed in 1979 was a commercial model — albeit a Leyland Marathon which Southall had been producing for the last four years of its existence.

It is sad that something so entirely British as AEC — Builders of London's Buses — should disappear, for they embodied the best of British engineering while the road transport enthusiast will miss the soft sound of the smooth running AEC engines, which over the years (with the exception of the V8) have proved so reliable, plus the peculiar and unique sounds of the AEC transmission with their worm driven rear axles. The marque has already virtually disappeared from everyday use on our roads, and it must be left to the valiant and dedicated band of enthusiasts who have preserved these wonderful vehicles to keep the memories alive and show the younger generation that Britain could deliver the goods!

This book like others in the series, is basically a pictorial record of the various models the company has produced, but as the AEC name has now departed it must also form a history of the company. While not intended to be a 'blow-by-blow' account of the politics and fortunes of AEC, it is hoped that the salient points have been covered.

The illustrations have all been taken from the Ian Allan Library, the majority of which are AEC official photographs, while others are from the author's own collection. The specifications of the various models have been obtained from the official AEC sales and publicity literature.

S. W. STEVENS-STRATTEN, FRSA
Epsom

1 Walthamstow 1912-1926

The Associated Equipment Company was formed on 13 June 1912, having its feet already firmly entrenched in the manufacture of London's buses. Four years earlier the London General Omnibus Company Ltd (General) had merged with the London Motor Omnibus Company Ltd (Vanguard) and the London Road Car Company (Union Jack) and thus there was a heterogeneous fleet of some 890 vehicles which needed servicing and replacing. The Chief Motor Engineer, Frank Searle, quickly realised that a purpose built and standardised vehicle would be more reliable and economic and thus persuaded his directors that the old Vanguard premises at Blackhorse Road, Walthamstow, used as a maintenance and service depot, should be reorganised as a production plant.

The first prototype bus was produced in August 1909 and was finally, after modification, approved by the Public Carriage Office of the Metropolitan Police, put into service in December 1909. This was known as the X type of which 60 where built (plus one lorry) and powered by a 28hp engine. The open top body seated 16 inside and 18 outside — nowadays known as the lower and upper decks respectively!

The X type proved to be the prototype for the more refined and very famous B type which followed and was in service from October 1910. The engine was a 30hp (later uprated) four-cylinder petrol engine driving a three-speed gearbox with a cone clutch and worm driven rear axle. The chassis had an ash frame and nickel-silver flitch plates which again carried a 34-seat body (16 inside and 18 outside).

Using an early form of production line or volume production, 30 chassis per week were being manufactured by 1912 and a total of 2,678 buses of the B type were built in three years, all within a factory whose total area was only 3,000sq ft. Many hundreds of the B type buses were commandeered for the 1914-18 war and saw service in France as exemplified by the preserved 'Ole Bill' in the London Transport Museum.

In 1912 the London General Omnibus Company had been taken over by the Underground Electric Railways Company of London Ltd (Underground), who decided as part of their reorganisation, that the vehicle manufacturing side of their empire should become a separate entity which, financed wholly by themselves with a share capital of £500,000, could produce and sell vehicles not only for their own requirements, but also to outside operators. The Walthamstow factory was sold to the new company for £85,000.

The first true commercial vehicle was produced in 1916 for having proved knowledgeable and experienced in large scale production, the government entrusted to AEC the task of manufacturing thousands of 3-4ton army trucks for the war effort. The result was the highly successful Y type, a robust and purpose built vehicle with a pressed steel frame and fitted with a 45hp four-cylinder petrol engine driving a four-speed crash gearbox. The heavy chassis enabled it to carry loads far in excess of its official rating, although it owed much of its design to the B type bus chassis of 1910. The vehicles were built on a moving track assembly line, believed to have been the first in Europe and one complete vehicle was rolled off the line every 30 minutes. By the end of 1918 more than 10,000 of the Y type vehicles had been built and supplied to the War Department who distributed them to all three Services.

By the end of the war in 1918 the factory space had increased from its original 3,000sq ft to a floor area of 483,000sq ft with new buses of the K type being produced along with a civilianised version of the Y type WD lorry. Classified as the YA model the normal control 4-wheeled lorry could carry loads of 3-5ton and options of Tylor, Daimler, or a few with AEC, engines of 45hp were fitted while there were variations in the length of wheelbase ranging from 14ft, 14ft 2¾in or 14ft 11in as the customer required. The various permutations being classified as YA, YB, YC, YD and YE types, later to become the 501 series. Production finished in 1921, although a 4ton tipper was exhibited at the 5th Motor Show at Olympia in that year

In 1923, AEC introduced a brand new vehicle, which proved highly successful and the forerunner of future developments, although, incidentally, the smallest commercial vehicle they ever produced. The 2/2½ton normal control chassis was known as the 201 type, featuring an AEC built 28hp, 4-cylinder wet-sleeve monobloc engine and a transmission type handbrake and wormdrive rear axle. The model developed into the 204 type and remained in production until 1928.

The financial situation which was affecting other manufacturers was also casting a shadow on AEC, as stated by the Right Hon Lord Ashfield, Chairman of the Underground Group of Companies, at their Annual General Meeting on 8 March 1923 at Caxton Hall, Westminster . . . 'I cannot speak in favourable terms of the Associated Equipment Company's present financial position. The stagnation in the motor trade, as in many other trades continues, and it is not made better by the considerable number of surplus war vehicles which still seek a market. Except for the manufacture of omnibuses required for the reinstatement and strengthening of the fleet employed in London, that company has found scanty opening for the sale of new vehicles. It has not been able to contribute anything to your income in this year under review (1922), but it has somewhat bettered its general financial position by writing down its stock and plant'. Such words could be true of many companies today, excepting the surplus WD vehicles!

In 1926 informed circles suggested that AEC should

leave the Underground control and become an independent company and negotiations had been commenced with Leyland Motors Ltd for a merger and a step towards rationalisation of the commercial vehicle industry. These preliminary transactions did not bear fruit, but in June of that year an agreement was reached with the Daimler Co Ltd of Coventry whereby their sleeve valve engines could be fitted to AEC chassis and there would be joint marketing of both firm's products under the name of Associated Daimler. This joint marketing lasted for only two years and in 1928 the companies resumed their separate ways with their own marketing, but many vehicles had been produced with the Associated Daimler name on the radiator.

During this time the AEC fortunes were rising and in 1925 they made a profit of £68,000, and the following year increased this to £129,447. With a brighter future ahead the company was somewhat hampered in production by the lack of space at Walthamstow, which had only started as a repair depot for buses and although it had been extended as demands required, they had literally run out of space added to which it was natural that the layout was not conducive to the large manufacturing plant that evolved, with much handling between the various buildings, all of which proved uneconomical.

A site for a brand new and enlarged custom-built factory was found at Southall in Middlesex where expansion and greater productivity could be achieved coupled with better working conditions where specially built machinery and service could be provided.

Specification for Type 201/204 normal control 2/2½ton chassis.
Engine: AEC 28hp 4-cylinder petrol 100mm bore by 140mm stroke. Monobloc construction with cylinder jacket and crankcase in one piece. Side valves and tappets carried in a separate casting removable through the side of the engine casing. Magneto ignition. Three point engine suspension.
Clutch: Inverted cone type with adjustable stop.
Gears:
1st ratio of 5.06:1 giving 2.93mph at 1,000rpm
2nd ratio of 2.79:1 giving 5.3mph at 1,000rpm
3rd ratio of 1.7:1 giving 8.74mph at 1,000rpm
4th direct giving 14.86mph at 1,000rpm
Reverse ratio of 6.32:1 giving 2.35mph at 1,000rpm.
Rear axle: Worm drive on roller bearings with 7.25:1 reduction.
Wheels & tyres: Steel castings with 920mm by 100mm solid tyres (twins at rear). Later pneumatic tyres of 36in by 6in could be fitted.
Chassis: Pressed steel 7in deep, straight and parallel with cross-members.
Chassis weight: 2ton 4cwt.
Wheelbase: 11ft 6in.
Overall length: 18ft 4in.
Overall width: 7ft 5½in.
Body space: 11ft long by 6ft 2in wide.
Frame height: 2ft 6in.
Ground clearance: 9¾in.
Fuel tank: 13gal petrol tank carried on dashboard.

Below:
One of the early commercial vehicles produced at Walthamstow. A lorry for the parent company — LGOC. It is on a B type bus chassis and even the body has the bus type cab.

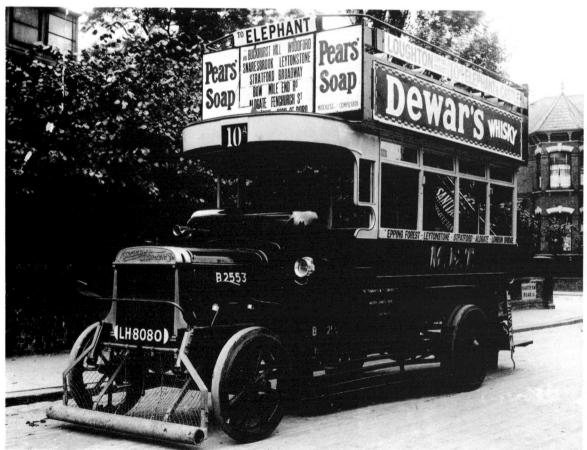

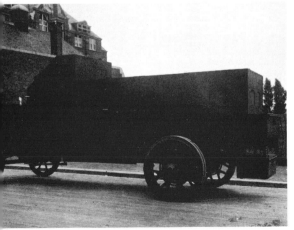

Far above left:
A van body on a B type bus chassis used by the Advertising Department of LGOC. Note their initials on the radiator header tank.

Far left:
B type bus supplied to the Metropolitan Electric Tramways Co, taken over by the LGOC in 1912 about the same time as AEC was formed. This shows the same radiator shell shape as shown in the previous photograph, but now bearing the words 'Associated Equipment Co Ltd' written out in full. The length of steel pipe and the chicken netting at the front is not an idea to smooth out bumps in the road! It is a lifeguard for prospective passengers should they walk into the road to board the oncoming bus as they did for a tram.

Left:
B type bus chassis converted into an armoured car for World War 1.

Above:
A standard Y type lorry, of which 10,000 were supplied to the War Department by 1919.

Left:
Y type lorry in service with the British Army.

Below left:
Lorry-bus converted from a WD Y type used by United Automobile Services just after the 1914-18 war. Note the registration number, as Norfolk County Council used the unorthodox practice of putting a zero in front of the figures.

Above:
Tylor engined Y type of 1919 and subsequently fitted with pneumatic tyres. Note the wooden planked door.

Below:
Little has been done to convert this Y type for civilian use apart from extending the sides with the lattice work.

Above and left:
Placed in service in 1919 by the Northampton Brewery this Y type 3tonner lorry is fitted with a 45hp Tylor engine. The vehicle is now preserved.

Above right:
Later in its life the Y type was redesignated the 501 model as shown here.

Right:
It would appear that this 501 model was never intended to be demonstrated at night as there is a complete absence of lights and even lamp brackets!

Right:
The smallest and lightest vehicle AEC ever produced. The 201 type for 2/2½ton loads was fitted with a 24.7hp petrol engine. This 1925 vehicle could also be supplied with pneumatic tyres at extra cost.

Below:
The 701 model was built as a tractive unit for an early experiment in articulation. The vehicle carried a Carrimore coupling and a tank bodied semi-trailer of the same make. The overall length of the unit was 33ft.

Bottom:
A scene at the Bank in London during the General Strike of 1926 depicting a convoy of AEC lorries with military personnel. The leading vehicle disappearing at the bottom left of the illustration is a Thornycroft. A large number of people seem to be doing precisely nothing!

2 Southall – The late 1920s

Construction of the new factory was commenced in 1926 and the move from Walthamstow to Southall completed in May and June 1927. The actual move was carried out by Pickfords Ltd who handled, over a period of three months, approx 10,000ton equally spread between plant and machinery, and stores. The only link with the old premises was the telegraphic address, which right to the end remained as 'Vangastow' — an amalgam of Vanguard and Walthamstow.

The new situation was a triangular shaped 63 acre site bounded on one side by the main line of the Great Western Railway, from which a private siding was connected giving direct access into the works; the Grand Union Canal and the final side by Windmill Lane, joining the main Uxbridge Road at the 'Iron Bridge' — notorious to motoring commuters as the location of rush-hour traffic jams! Thus the new premises had access to rail, road and water transport and incorporated their own vehicle test track including a gradient. Soon the names of AEC and Southall became synonymous.

The Southall plant had been designed in the first instance for an output of not less than 150 chassis per week and production of the type 201/204 2/2½tonner, as well as four different bus chassis proceeded with the introduction in mid-1927 of another new commercial chassis. This was the 418 model for 3½ton payloads, later increased to 4ton as model 418/1, which was a normal control or cab-behind-engine layout. Fitted with a 38-45hp four-cylinder petrol engine, production of this model lasted until 1930 and they became available with either solid or pneumatic tyres.

Following quickly on the heels of the 418 model another chassis was produced in 1928 known as the 506 (also called Granville) which was to fill the gap left by the Y or 501 type. This new vehicle was again a normal control model for 4/5ton payloads and this proved popular with many operators, some even being used for passenger bodywork with a maximum of 36 seats.

At the same time as the bonneted 506 model appeared a larger forward control (cab-over-engine) was introduced for 6ton payloads and this was the 507 type which for a time was named Ramillies. Fitted with a 45hp petrol engine and a totally enclosed cab, its angular appearance made it look massive by the standards of the day, but it does not appear to have sold in large numbers due to its heavy unladen weight and the old Y type gearbox. The model was shortly superseded by the new Mammoth.

Enjoying a greater popularity was the 428 model which carried a 4ton payload with full forward control which was introduced in mid-1928. It was a surprisingly nippy vehicle and from test reports of the time it appeared to handle very well. Several of the components were identical to the 418 model, including the engine, gearbox and transmission. The upper half of the forward control cab was arranged to hinge backwards so that easy access could be gained to the engine.

Another short wheelbase model was a variation of the 506 and 507 models and numbered as 508. This had the driver alongside the engine and was for a 5ton payload which was later uprated to 6ton and the model numbered as 508/1.

Within a year one of the largest chassis for commercial vehicles was offered to operators which could also accommodate a 54 seat passenger body as well as one for a 6ton payload. Designated the 509 it was a forward control type again placing the driver alongside the engine. The well proven four-cylinder poppet valve engine of 45hp was used and gears and transmission were similar to the other models produced at this time. It is interesting to note that the chassis cost £925 complete.

Around 1928 pneumatic tyres were becoming both reliable and acceptable and thus models produced from this time were offered with a choice of solids or 'pump-ups'.

In June 1928 two appointments were made by AEC, the first that Lieut-Col J. T. C. Moore-Brabazon, MP (later to become Lord Brabazon of Tara) be appointed a director, and the second that G. J. Rackham be appointed Chief Engineer and Designer. Mr Rackham, who had previously been with LGOC and AEC had left to undertake transport work in America, later returning to the UK and joining Leyland. He was to revolutionise the AEC designs within a space of 15 months and there can be little doubt that it was his influence that put AEC on the top level of commercial vehicle manufacturers.

Another sign of consolidation and expansion was made in October 1928 when agreement was reached with the Four Wheel Drive, England (including Hardy Rail Motors Ltd) whereby that company would use AEC components in their range of cross-country vehicles. In 1931 the FWD company changed their name to avoid confusion with their parent organisation in the USA and in the same year production of their vehicles moved to Southall.

After the marketing agreement with Daimler had finished in 1928, the Daimler concern tried to obtain contracts for the supply of London buses, and therefore AEC made another but more specific proposal to Leyland Motors that they formed a joint holding company, British Vehicles, both with equal shares, to secure a seven year contrast for the supply of bus chassis for London. However, after preliminary negotiations the proposal was abandoned and eventually AEC was awarded the contract on their own.

Specification for Type 418 and 418/1 normal control 3½-4ton chassis
Engine: AEC four-cylinder 108mm bore by 140mm

stroke, 35-45hp at 1,000rpm. RAC rating 29hp. Magneto ignition.

Clutch: Fabric covered inverted cone.

Gears:

1st ratio of 5.06:1 giving 2.95mph at 1,000rpm (on solids)

2nd ratio of 2.97:1 giving 5.02mph at 1,000rpm (on solids)

3rd ratio of 1.7:1 giving 8.76mph at 1,000rpm (on solids)

4th direct giving 14.9mph at 1,000rpm (on solids).

Reverse ratio of 6.32:1 giving 2.36mph at 1,000rpm (on solids)

Rear axle: Worm drive giving 7.25:1 reduction.

Brakes: Both foot and handbrake operate only on rear drums.

Wheels and tyres: Steel castings with 920mm by 120mm solids (twins at rear) for 771mm rims or 38in by 7in pneumatics (twins at rear).

Chassis: Pressed steel parallel with cross members.

Chassis weight: 2ton 13cwt.

Wheelbase: 13ft 6in.

Overall length: 21ft 8in.

Overall width: 6ft 7$\frac{1}{4}$in.

Body space: 13ft 6in.

Frame height: 2ft 5$\frac{1}{2}$in.

Ground clearance: 9$\frac{1}{2}$in.

Fuel tank: 35 gallon petrol tank longitudinally under driver's seat.

Specification for Type 506 normal control 4/5ton chassis

Engine: AEC four-cylinder petrol 120mm bore by 150mm stroke, 45hp at 1,000rpm. Magneto ignition and Zenith carburettor.

Clutch: Ferrodo lined inverted cone of large diameter with adjuster spring and stop.

Gears:

1st ratio of 5.12:1 giving 2.76mph at 1,000rpm

2nd ratio of 2.98:1 giving 4.98mph at 1,000rpm

3rd ratio of 1.69:1 giving 8.33mph at 1,000rpm

4th ratio of Direct giving 14.08mph at 1,000rpm

Reverse ratio of 5.12:1 giving 2.76mph at 1,000rpm.

Rear axle: Worm drive giving reduction of 8.5:1.

Brakes: Foot and handbrake operating on rear drums only.

Wheels and tyres: Steel castings with 1,010mm rims for 140mm by 850mm (twins at rear).

Chassis: High tensile steel 8$\frac{5}{8}$in deep by 9/32in thick, parallel with cross members.

Chassis weight: 3ton 9cwt.

Wheelbase: 14ft.

Overall length: 22ft 6$\frac{1}{4}$in.

Overall width: 7ft 1$\frac{3}{4}$in.

Body space: 15ft 0$\frac{1}{2}$in.

Ground clearance: 11in.

Fuel tank: 30 gallon under driver's seat

Specification for Type 428 forward control 4ton — where different from 418

Wheelbase: 10ft 6in.

Overall length: 18ft 10$\frac{3}{4}$in.

Body space: 14ft 6in.

Specification for Type 508 forward control 5ton — where different from 506

Chassis weight: 2ton 10cwt.

Wheelbase: 12ft 6in.

Overall length: 20ft.

Body space: 14ft 6in.

Specification for Type 509 forward control 6ton where different from 508

Wheels and tyres: 1,010mm by 160mm solids (twins at rear)

Chassis weight: 3ton 12cwt

Wheelbase: 15ft 9$\frac{1}{2}$in.

Overall length: 25ft 6in.

Overall width: 7ft 1$\frac{1}{2}$in.

Body space: 19ft 4in.

Below left:
A model 428 lorry of 1928 which carries the name 'Associated Equipment' written in full on the radiator shell. Compare this with the van shown at bottom of this page.

Above:
A model 506 with a van type body specially constructed for the carriage of two 1,000 light gas meters. The rear half of the body has a sliding cover to facilitate loading. This was one of three vehicles supplied and has a body length of 14ft, a width of 7ft 6in and internal headroom of 7ft.

Above right:
Another 506 model operated by a Middlesex brewery for transporting crates of beer. The vehicle had completed over 2,000 miles within a few weeks of purchase and is shown here on a typical delivery.

Right:
Another model of a 428, this one a short wheelbase van also manufactured in 1928, but carrying the name 'Associated Daimler' in full on the same radiator shell as the lorry opposite. The initials 'ADC' appear on the hubcaps.

Overleaf:

Above:
Chassis diagram for model 418.

Below:
Chassis diagram for model 508.

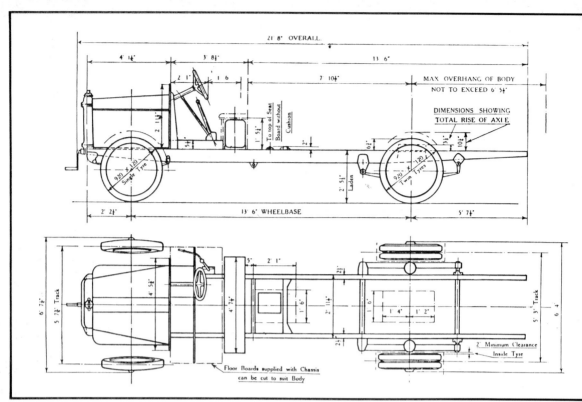

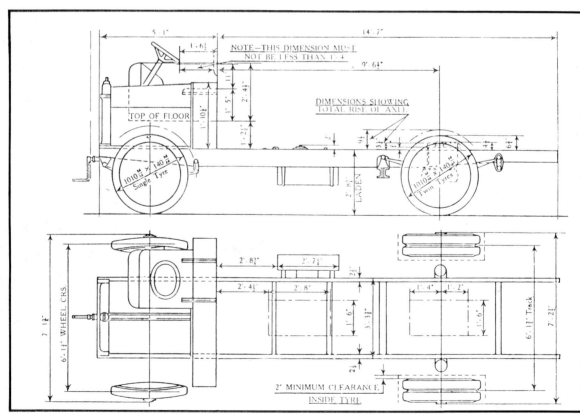

3 Southall - The 1930s

Between 1929-32 AEC redesigned its entire range of both commercial and bus chassis (the later introducing the Regal and Regent names) and thus took their biggest step to establish their name in the forefront of heavy vehicle production in the UK. This was entirely due to the clever and ingenious designs of John Rackham for the old heavyweight designs were replaced by light alloy components, such as transmission casings, which gave better power to weight ratio and proved far more economical to the operator on mileage and fuel consumption. He used many parts which were common to other vehicles in the range and they attained an enviable reputation for reliability and with only minor modifications the 1930 models continued without many major outward changes until the 1950s.

All the new models displayed the now familiar AEC triangular badge for the first time, and this incorporated the older style logo with the AEC being set in a straight oblong box breaking across a circle, similar to the logo used by the LGOC and London Transport, who were still in control of AEC. Whether the use of the triangle was meant to represent the shape of the Southall site is not known.

The initial success of the new range meant that the Southall factory had to be expanded and thus in October 1930 the capital was raised to £1.5m by issuing 40,000 denomination shares of £10 each.

The four new goods chassis were the Mercury, a normal control 3½ton; the Monarch, a forward control 4ton; the Majestic, a normal control for 6ton loads and the biggest of the range, at that date, the Mammoth a forward control for 7-8ton payload. A new type of fully enclosed all metal cab with sliding side windows was fitted and this gave the vehicles a lighter, smoother and speedier appearance. The inverted cone type clutch previously used on all models was now replaced by a single plate clutch of 16in diameter.

The two smallest vehicles in the range — Mercury and Monarch shared the same 4-cylinder overhead valve AEC petrol engine which with a bore of 112mm by 130mm stroke developed 38bhp at 1,000rpm and 65bhp at 2,000rpm (RAC rating 31.1hp). Gear ratios and back axle ratings were also similar. On test a Monarch touched 60mph with a full load on level ground and averaged 8.9mpg for fuel consumption. The Mercury continued in production until 1937, but the Monarch was updated and re-rated in 1934.

The other two new vehicles — Majestic and Mammoth — shared a larger engine which was an AEC overhead valve petrol engine and six-cylinders of 110mm bore by 130mm stroke developing 110bhp at 2,000rpm (45hp on RAC rating). The Mammoth was capable of 50mph with full load on level ground, while both the vehicles could pull a drawbar trailer with a 5ton load. The Majestic was produced for six years, but the Mammoth was changed in 1935.

A big breakthrough with far reaching consequences occurred in 1930/31 when, after two years of continued research and development, AEC produced their first high speed oil (or diesel) engine. This entirely new engine was designed from inception to give a wide speed range with flexibility, smooth running and clean exhaust. At that time oil was much cheaper than petrol and John Rackhams new engine accounted in no small measure to the success of the range, despite the initial reluctance on the part of operators and customers to avail themselves of the option and sample its efficiency and economy. It is a tribute to its design that within a space of a couple of years over one fifth of all orders specified the oil engine to be fitted and a few years later the petrol engined AEC vehicles were virtually obsolete.

The new engine was not, as in so many other cases, a conversion of an existing unit. It had six-cylinders of 115mm bore by 142mm stroke which equalled 8.1litres and with a compression ratio of 16:1 developed 140bhp at 2,500rpm. Fuel consumption for a 5ton laden lorry was 10mpg. The engine, which had a one-piece cylinder block and a seven bearing crankshaft, was entirely British made with the exception of the Bosch fuel pump and injectors and with 24V electric starter motor the weight of the engine was 1,414lb.

Three entirely new models appeared for the 1932 production programme. First was the Matador, a forward control 5ton chassis which had many similarities with the existing Mercury model, including the same engine. Next was the Mandator (Model 669) which was a heavy duty forward control 6ton chassis resembling the Regent double deck bus chassis which enabled a low loading height to be obtained with an offset double reduction bevel type rear axle and this remained in production until 1935/6. Last of the new models was a development of the Mammoth four wheeler introduced the previous year but now offered as a six-wheeled chassis and named the Mammoth Major 6 (Model 668) capable of carrying loads up to 12ton.

In the same year an articulated unit which could be coupled to a Carrimore semi-trailer was introduced. This was the standard Mammoth chassis but shortened to a wheelbase of 10ft 6in so that the legal limit of maximum length of 33ft could be kept but it enabled a body space of 25ft 6in to be available. It was not really successful as operators at that time were very wary of articulated units and considered the difficulties of reversing them as a sufficient deterrent.

With an eye to the export market the Marshal (only one 'l' is correct!) six-wheel model 673 was introduced in July 1932. This was for 3-5ton loads using the four-cylinder 80bhp engine with four-speed gearbox and two-speed auxiliary box. This was a result of the AEC/Hardy merger as the latter concern produced the four-wheel drive rear bogie, which incidentally, had a $9\frac{3}{4}$in axle rise on either side.

Meanwhile in 1933 the formation of the London Passenger Transport Board made it necessary to distribute the assets of AEC and the share capital was distributed to the Underground shareholders and thus AEC was converted into a public company.

Since the introduction of the 8litre oil engine two years earlier, research and progress had been maintained and therefore in 1934 a 130hp six-cylinder engine of 8.85litres had been developed. This featured the AEC-Ricardo Comet design of combustion chamber which not only improved the performance but virtually eliminated the familiar diesel knock at all but the slowest speeds. The engine proved as versatile as, and almost indistinguishable from, the petrol unit. Hand-in-hand with this development was the introduction of a four-cylinder diesel engine of 5.35litre and 6.7litre capacity developing 70bhp and 85bhp respectively at 2,000rpm. Both versions remained in production until 1940.

In 1935 further progress had been made with the six-cylinder engine and now with a 7.7litre capacity and lighter in weight with the same power output this now superseded the 8.8litre engine and it more or less remained unchanged for the next 20 years. The design featured twin cast-iron cylinder heads and a camshaft high up in the main block with short push-rods. The high position of the camshaft enabled a simple layout for the timing chain with the auxiliaries driven from this. Two years later the Comet combustion chambers were replaced with direct injection.

One of the most popular of all AEC models was introduced in February 1934 and this was the Mammoth Major 8 for 14-14$\frac{1}{2}$ton payloads and a logical development of the Mammoth Major 6. First numbered as model 680 this was changed in 1936 to model 386 but it remained basically the same vehicle but given the suffix Mk II. The Ministry of Transport at that time permitted a gross weight of 22ton for eight-wheelers and allowed them to travel at the legal maximum of 20mph. Fuel consumption of the Mammoth Major 8 averaged 7.25mpg with full load over 14$\frac{1}{2}$miles at an average of 18mph.

Also in 1934 the Monarch Mk II was produced and this was the lightest 7-8tonner on the market. Coded as model 344 it still had the straight frame chassis but its fuel consumption averaged 9.17mpg at an average speed of 20mph.

By 1935 the Mk II versions of the Matador, Mercury, Mammoth Major 6 and Mammoth Major 8 were appearing. Generally speaking there was little change in outward appearance, but most of the Mk II models were lighter in weight, the saving being on the chassis and the fitting of the newer engines. There was also a choice of several different wheelbase lengths and often a choice of two engines, and rear axle ratios.

In 1937 (regarded as a 1938 model) AEC met the demand for a vehicle between the rigid maximum load four-wheeler and the heavy duty six-wheeler by introducing the Mammoth Minor (model 366) for 10ton loads. This had a single tyre trailing the normal twin tyred rear axle. The model was built up to 1940 but was not continued after the war as were the other ranges.

At the outbreak of the war AEC produced a twin-steer three-axle chassis as an alternative to the Mammoth Minor and one presumes the new model was similarly rated for a gross weight of 16ton or a payload of 10-10$\frac{1}{2}$ton. Fitted with the six-cylinder 7.7litre engine and standard four-speed gearbox it had 9.75×20 tyres all round with twins on the rear axle.

At the end of the 1930s many of the vehicles were powered with the AEC-Ricardo 7.7litre direct injection, six-cylinder oil engine which with a bore of 105mm and a stroke of 146mm developed 102bhp at 1,750rpm.

Specification for Mercury (Type 640) normal control 3$\frac{1}{2}$ton chassis.
Engine: AEC four-cylinder overhead valve petrol 112mm bore by 130mm stroke giving 65bhp at 2,000rpm.
Clutch: Single plate 16in dia with adjusting stop.
Gears:
1st ratio of 4.37:1 giving 7.1mph at 2,000rpm
2nd ratio of 2.69:1 giving 11.6mph at 2,000rpm
3rd ratio of 1.59:1 giving 19.2mph at 2,000rpm
4th direct giving 31.2mph at 2,000rpm
Reverse ratio of 5.33:1 giving 5.9mph at 2,000rpm.
Rear axle: Overhead worm, standard reduction 7.25:1.
Brakes: Servo assisted foot brake to all four wheels. Handbrake operates on rear wheels only. Rear drums 17in dia.
Wheels and tyres: Tyres 34×7 (twins on rear). 940mm×140mm solids if required.
Chassis: Straight and parallel 8in deep by 3in wide nickel-steel pressings $\frac{5}{16}$in thick.
Chassis weight: 2ton 17cwt.
Wheelbase: 14ft.
Overall length: 20ft 5in.
Overall width: 7ft 4$\frac{1}{4}$in.
Body space: 14ft.
Frame height: 2ft 8in.
Ground clearance: 10$\frac{1}{4}$in.
Fuel: 35gal tank under driver's seat.

Specification for Monarch (Type 641) forward control 4ton chassis where different from Mercury
Wheels and tyres: 38×7 (twins on rear). 940mm×140mm solids if required.
Chassis weight: 2ton 18cwt.
Wheelbase: 13ft.
Overall length: 18ft 7in.
Fuel: 35gal tank on chassis frame.

Specification for Majestic (Type 666) normal control 6ton chassis
Engine: AEC six-cylinder overhead valve petrol 110mm bore by 130mm stroke giving 56bhp at 1,000rpm and 110bhp at 2,000rpm.
Clutch: Single plate 16in dia.

Gears:
1st ratio of 4.37:1 giving 6.1mph at 2,000rpm (standard axle)
2nd ratio of 2.69:1 giving 10mph at 2,000rpm (standard axle)
3rd ratio of 1.59:1 giving 16.8mph at 2,000rpm (standard axle)
4th direct giving 27.1mph at 2,000rpm (standard axle)
Reverse ratio of 5.33 giving 5mph at 2,000rpm (standard axle).
Rear axle: Double reduction 9.3:1 standard (other options available).
Brakes: Servo assisted footbrake on all four wheels. Handbrake on rear only. Rear drums 20in dia, Front drums 17in dia.
Wheels and tyres: 40×8 (twins on rear). Pneumatics are standard.
Chassis: Straight and parallel 10in deep by 3in wide. Nickel-steel pressing of $^5/_{16}$in thick.
Chassis weight: 3ton 12cwt.
Wheelbase: 16ft 7in.
Overall length: 24ft 11in.
Overall width: 7ft 4$\frac{1}{4}$in.
Body space: 16ft 6in.
Frame height: 3ft.
Ground clearance: 11in.
Fuel: 50gal tank

Specification for Mammoth (Type 667) forward control 7-8ton chassis where different from Majestic

Wheels and tyres: 42×9 (twins on rear). Pneumatics as standard. 1,010mm by 180mm solids if required.
Chassis weight: 4ton.
Body space: 20ft.

Specification for Matador (Type 645) forward control 5ton chassis where different from Mercury

Rear axle: Double reduction 8:1 ratio.
Wheels and tyres: 40×8 (twins on rear) or 36×8 (twins on rear).
Chassis weight: 3ton 15cwt.
Wheelbase: 14ft 6in (or 12ft 1in or 16ft 7in as options).
Overall length: 22ft 6in.
Overall width: 7ft 5$\frac{1}{2}$in.
Body space: 17ft 6in.

Specification for Mandator (Type 669) forward control 5ton chassis

Engine: AEC six-cylinder overhead valve petrol 110mm bore by 130mm stroke giving 56bhp at 1,000rpm.
Clutch: Single plate 16in dia.
Gears: As Mercury or Majestic.
Rear axle: Offset double reduction.
Brakes: Servo assisted.
Wheels and tyres: 40×8 (twins at rear).

Chassis: Resembling Regent double-deck.
Chassis weight: 4ton 9cwt.
Wheelbase: 16ft 6in.
Overall length: 25ft 3$\frac{1}{2}$in.
Body space: 20ft 5in.
Fuel: 45gal tank.

Specification for Mammoth Major 6 (Type 668) forward control 12ton chassis

Engine: AEC six-cylinder overhead valve petrol or AEC six-cylinder oil engine 115mm bore by 142mm stroke 140bhp at 2,500rpm.
Clutch: Single plate 16in dia.
Gears:
1st ratio of 6.91:1 giving 5.26mph at 2,400rpm with 8:1 axle
2nd ratio of 4.25:1 giving 8.57mph at 2,400rpm with 8:1 axle
3rd ratio of 2.51:1 giving 14.5mph at 2,400rpm with 8:1 axle
4th ratio of 1.58:1 giving 23mph at 2,400rpm with 8:1 axle
5th direct giving 36.4mph at 2,400rpm with 8:1 axle
Reverse ratio of 8.41:1 giving 4.33mph at 2,400rpm with 8:1 axle.
Rear axle: Fully floating double reduction 8:1 (standard ratio).
Brakes: On rear only 20in drums.
Wheels and tyres: 40×8 (twins on rear).
Chassis: Straight and parallel 12in deep by 3$\frac{1}{2}$in wide of nickel-silver pressing $^5/_{16}$in thick.
Chassis weight: 5ton 18cwt.
Wheelbase: 16ft 10$\frac{1}{2}$in (or 14ft 10$\frac{1}{2}$in).
Overall length: 27ft 7in (or 23ft 5in).
Body space: 22ft 6in (or 19ft 6in) by 7ft 6in.
Ground clearance: 16in (10in under rear bogie).

Specification for Mammoth Major 8 (Type 680) forward control 14$\frac{1}{2}$ton chassis

Engine: As Mammoth Major 6.
Clutch: As Mammoth Major 6.
Gears:
1st ratio of 4.38:1 giving 5.25mph at 2,400rpm
2nd ratio of 2.96:1 giving 8.57mph at 2,400rpm
3rd ratio of 1.59:1 giving 14.5mph at 2,400rpm
4th direct giving 23mph at 2,400rpm
Reverse ratio: 5.3:1
Rear axle: Fully floating double reduction spiral bevel.
Brakes: 20in dia drums front and rear.
Wheels and tyres: 40×8 (twins on rear) (or 9.75×20 or 36×8).
Chassis: As Mammoth Major 6.
Wheelbase: 17ft 9$\frac{1}{2}$in.
Overall length: 27ft 10in.
Body space: 22ft 6in by 7ft 6in.

Left:
A Mercury (Model 640) 3½ton normal control tanker, which is one of 10 supplied to Anglo-American Oil Co Ltd in 1930 for petroleum deliveries.

Below left:
A model 641 Monarch 4ton short wheelbase van. Note the sliding doors at the rear side of the body for easy loading. This was one of eight supplied to the Danish Bacon Co in 1930/31.

Below:
Two Majestics, model 666 chassis with 1,500gal tank bodies outside the Burnley Road Garage, Accrington premises of their owners who had them on contract hire to Texaco. The aggregate mileage for the two vehicles in their first year of operation was 86,000 miles.

Right:
A 1930 built 6ton Majestic in the service of a well-known brewer. A similar vehicle was rebuilt during the war — see page 37.

Below right:
Bonneted Majestic tip lorry of 1931. Note the solid tyres at the rear and the pneumatics on the front.

Left:
In 1932 this Mercury 4ton, 1,000gal tanker visited 175 towns in the UK when supplying fuel for Sir Alan Cobham's air displays.

Below left:
Monarch 4ton lorry supplied in 1930/31 but fitted with solid tyres at the owner's request. Note the cast front wheels.

Above:
The shape of the AEC cab for many years to come. This 1932 Mammoth dropside lorry had red lettering on stone coloured bodywork.

Below:
Another 1932 Mammoth dropside lorry. This one is delivering materials for relaying the tram tracks in Wood Green, London.

MERCURY CHASSIS

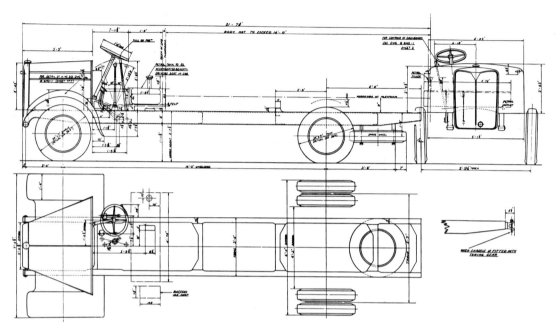

MONARCH CHASSIS

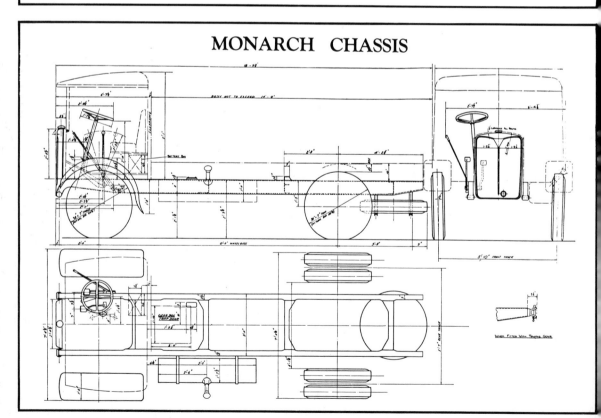

26

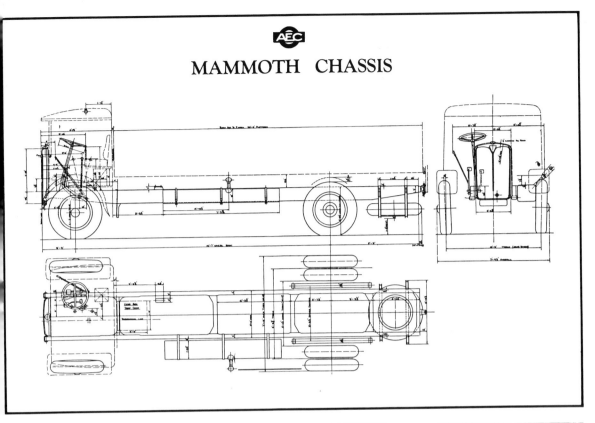

![AEC logo]

MAMMOTH CHASSIS

Above left:
Chassis diagram for Mercury, model 640.

Left:
Chassis diagram for Monarch, model 641.

Above:
Chassis diagram for Mammoth, model 667.

Right:
A 1932 Monarch chassis and trailer, both carrying wooden bodies for the conveyance of meat, mainly carcases to the retail butcher.

Below right:
An early version of the Mammoth Major supplied to the Burnley Co-operative Society in 1932.

Above right:
One of the early customers for the new Mammoth Major (Model 668) in 1932 was Hays Wharf Cartage Co Ltd who had a special Duramin body which was equipped to deal with both fresh and frozen food supplies.

Right:
This Mercury 4ton van (Model 640) was built in 1932 and has now been preserved.

Below:
This 1932 Mandator chassis has a 1,500gal tank body by W. P. Butterfield of Shipley. The streamlined appearance is gained by enclosing the tank fittings with aluminium panels.

Above left:
To obtain the extra space needed, many operators used a bus chassis for bulky but light loads. This pantechnicon of 1931 is based on the AEC Reliance single-deck bus or coach chassis.

Left:
A Monarch normal control model supplied in 1933 with container type lift-off body. Special attention has been given to the visibility from the cab hence the deep windscreen and low windows on the cab sides.

Below:
Another case where a psv chassis has been used for a commercial body. In this case a 1934 Ranger has been fitted with a 1,500gal tank body by Thompson Bros (Bilston) Ltd, who also included a sunshine roof for the driver's cab. The vehicle is powered by a 7.7litre AEC/Ricardo oil engine developing 126bhp. The wheelbase is 19ft long.

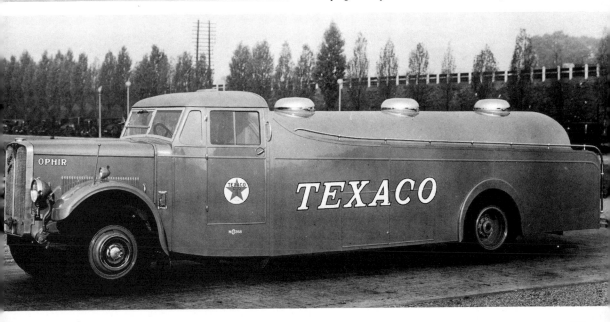

Above:
Another Ranger chassis was used two years later to convey 900
gallons of glucose. In this case the bodywork was undertaken by
Butterfields of Shipley.

Right:
A 1934 vehicle which fortunately has been preserved. This 0645
model Mandator has been owned throughout its life by Hall &
Co carrying builders materials, etc. It is seen here on the
Historic Commercial Vehicle Club's annual run to Brighton in
1967.

Below right:
The Mammoth Major 8 was introduced in 1934 and one of the
first customers was Charles W. Hewson who used this van on
contract hire. Fitted with an oil engine and a special lightweight
Duramin Engineering Co body the vehicle could carry a 15ton
payload.

Above:
Four Mercury's supplied to the Watford Co-operative Society in 1935 and only two have the same type of cab.

Left:
A normal control oil-engined six-wheeler poses outside Windsor Castle before delivering a new road roller to the local council in 1935.

Below:
One of two tractor trains supplied to the USSR in 1935. Each train has a maximum gross weight of 30ton and comprises the eight-wheeled, oil engined tractor unit and three Dyson built trailers — a hopper for grain, a 2,500gal tanker and a hand operated side tipper. A year earlier a similar type of train had been exported to the Gold Coast.

Above:
One of three special vehicles supplied to Pickfords in 1935 to
carry an 18ton load. They were used for carrying heavy loads
yet keeping within the legal limit regarding weight and
dimensions. The chassis consisted of heavy rolled steel joists.
The unladen weight was 7ton 16cwt, while the overall length
was 30ft. The height above ground was only 2ft. All wheels were
fitted with 12.75×20 low pressure single tyres. A six-cylinder,
110bhp oil engine was fitted.

Right:
A Mercury chassis used for London Transport Trolleybus
overhead maintenance work and supplied in 1937.

Above left and left:
An AEC Monarch petrol engined 'Ideal' refuse collector. Rear loading is at a constant height by rotation of the 22cu yd container. Tipping takes 20 seconds and rotating 27 seconds. The vehicle could also hold 1,100gal of water or decontamination fluid, delivered through a 3in centrifugal pump, for Air Raid Precautions (Civil Defence) work if required.

Below:
This Matador oil engined van has a 20ft long body yet weighs under 5ton unladen. It was one of six delivered in 1938 and each regularly pulled a laden four-wheel trailer.

Above:
Among the prewar exports were these two Monarch normal control tippers for the Water Conservation Irrigation Commission of Sydney, Australia.

Right:
The oil-engined Mammoth Major 8 had become popular with all operators. This sheeted tilt sided lorry was delivered in late 1935 and typifies the prewar AEC models.

Below:
A typical example of an immediate prewar production. A Mammoth Major 8 with tanker body.

4 The War Years

AEC, in common with the rest of British industry, had been tooling up for 12 months before the outbreak of World War 2 in September 1939. The main factory building covering an area of 14 acres on the 65 acre site was declared a 'Protected Place' within a matter of hours of War being officially declared and it was then subject to the Official Secrets Act. Civilian vehicle production was, with a very few exceptions, suspended immediately and the first and most important wartime commitment was for the Matador four-wheel drive medium artillery tractors.

This vehicle had its true origins 10 years before as a Hardy cross-country vehicle and the AEC continuous production lines were stretched to the utmost to produce as many as humanly possible. With a vast number of highly skilled personnel already called into HM Forces the labour shortage became a source of constant anxiety, while many of the designers and management were already on loan to various Government departments. However, in conjunction with the Ministry of Labour the factory was soon training both men and women in the necessary skills for vehicle production, plus running technical courses for other trades. By the end of the war just over 5,000 new employees were recruited from people not required for other national duties.

Another problem was the shortages of supplies for essential raw materials, plus the ever present risk of poor quality and substitute materials, which threw a considerable strain on the already depleted laboratories and inspection departments.

To add to the problems AEC, at the request of the Ministry of Supply took over a shadow factory at Park Royal where an entirely new production plant had to be installed to produce components for all types of vehicles required by HM Forces. The factory closed just before the end of the war but not before it had been damaged by a Flying Bomb (V1) which had landed close by.

The importance which the Germans attached to the AEC works was confirmed after the war when enemy maps and photographs of the installation, plus pilot's instructions even showing the position of anti-aircraft guns, were unearthed. Although several attacks were made on the Southall factory the worst was on the night of 24 September 1940 when a bomb was dropped on the Service Department. Fortunately the night shift workers were already in nearby shelters and nobody was injured, but damage to the building was extensive. At other times bombs, incendiary bombs, flying bombs and even rockets (V2) caused other superficial damage — broken windows and roofs — but no major damage was inflicted and work carried on as normal — even if in draughty conditions!

The AEC Matador four-wheel drive gun tractor (model 0853) was first built in 1937 having a gross weight of 10½ton with a load capacity of 3½ton and powered by the 7.7litre oil engine. It was given a test with other military vehicles, but it took Army engineers a few months before they fully appreciated its capabilities and then after further extended trials of hauling gun carriages over cross-country terrain it was accepted and an initial order for 200 given. When war was declared production went into full swing, the vehicle being regarded by all ranks of the Army, from Commander-in-Chief to the humble driver, as the 'best tractor in the medium class in either of the opposing armies'. It hauled the 3.7in heavy anti-aircraft guns in the UK and other spheres of operation, while abroad it also towed the 5.5in howitzer and the 7.5in field gun in practically every battlefield.

Having established itself in no uncertain terms the variations and uses soon became commonplace and the next special design was the Armoured Command Vehicle which was equipped with commodious fully armoured bodywork containing office furniture and other acoutrements needed as mobile battle headquarters for military commanders in the field.

The RAF also found the Matador suitable for hauling trailers as well as a general service vehicle and a large number of platform bodied types were delivered, initially with petrol engines but later the RAF found that diesel engines had advantages and thus the standard Matador was employed.

The next order was for approx 150 basically Matadors with armour-plated cabs and a flat platform body on which was mounted a swivelling turret with a six-pounder gun for the North African campaign and quickly known as 'Yellow Devils' as they were so painted to blend in with the sandy terrain. They were also often used to tow disabled tanks back to base workshops.

The needs of the RAF for refuellers (or bowsers) capable of carrying 2,500gal of fuel caused the AEC to produce a cross between the Matador and the Marshal — model 0854. The front of the former was coupled to the rear of the latter although this was virtually obsolete as it had the old three-quarter floating shafts instead of the more modern fully floating rear axles. Dual drive through the rear bogie thus gave a rigid 6×6 vehicle which, with a power winch fitted as standard, could exert a pull of 7ton and with low auxiliary gear this 6×6 could pull almost anything — anywhere, including the recovery of crash-landed aircraft. Some of these chassis were also fitted with Coles Cranes capable of lifting up to 10ton.

AEC were also developing a 6×6 gun tractor of low height, but before production commenced the allies had gained supremacy and the need for the vehicles was countermanded.

As well as conventional commercial vehicles, albeit to War Department specifications etc, AEC developed many special vehicles such as the armoured car. First produced as a private venture the mock-up was seen by high-ranking army officers and the Prime Minister (The Right

Hon Winston Churchill), and production authorised. The Mk I version (model 0855) was powered by the well-proven 7.7litre oil engine and carried a two-pounder gun and a BSA .303in (7.92mm) light machine gun. The Mk II and Mk III versions (model 0856) were fitted with the 9.6 direct injection oil engine as used in Valentine tanks and carried a six-pounder or 75mm gun. The engines of all the armoured cars were positioned at the rear and mounted inclined to obtain a lower height. The Mk III had steel plating up to $1\frac{1}{4}$in thick which made the weight of the vehicle in working order 12ton 14cwt. It could travel at 43mph on roads or at 18mph in rough country. The wheelbase was 11ft $4\frac{3}{4}$in, overall length 17ft $9\frac{3}{4}$in, width 8ft $10\frac{1}{2}$in and laden height 8ft 10in. Many of the vehicles were waterproofed for the D-Day landings.

AEC also undertook considerable development and experimental work for various Ministries and government departments and one such project was the flail tank for destroying enemy mines. The basic idea was a revolving drum on which chains were attached which beat the ground in front of the vehicle. The flails were driven by an outside auxiliary engine for two types of tank — the Matilda and Valentine, which were known as Baron and Scorpion respectively. When the flails were fitted to Sherman tanks they were driven by a take-off from the main engines — usually five Chryslers. Production of the flail tanks was undertaken by outside firms once AEC had perfected the design.

One of the deadliest weapons developed by AEC, in conjunction with the Petroleum Warfare Department,

was the flame-thrower which could devastate armour, buildings and, unfortunately, human beings in a holocaust of fire. The first one was developed and built on a Marshal 6×6 chassis and later designs were placed on armoured cars and tanks. Later a flame throwing trailer for towing was developed and called 'Crocodile'.

Among other wartime activities was the supply of diesel-electric sets for Mulberry Harbour used to embark the allied troops in Northern France on D-Day (6 June 1944). AEC stationary engines were also used in many other operations such as the 100ft underground dynamo built at Chatham in 1939. The company also built 381 pairs of twin oil engines and 353 petrol engines (140bhp) for Matilda tanks and 3,254 oil engines (9.6litre) for Valentine tanks.

Through its subsidiary, British Gear Grinding & Manufacturing Co, AEC produced gears for the Rolls-Royce Merlin, the Griffon engines and also the Napier Sabre engines.

The AEC wartime achievements can be summarised by the following list:

Matador gun tractor (models 853/0853)	8,61
RAF Matador float lorries	41
Matador Armoured Command Vehicles	41
Armoured Gun Carriers (6pdr gun) based on Matador	17
Armoured cars (models 0855 and 0856)	62
Marshal 2,500gal refuelling tanks for RAF (model 854/0854)	1,51
Marshal 6×6 lorries	60
Marshal 6×6 mobile oxygen plants	18
Marshal 6×6 chassis with Coles cranes for RAF	19
Marshal 6×6 Armoured Command Vehicles (model 0857)	15
Experimental flame throwers	
AEC 6×6 experimental gun tractor	
	12,89

A very limited number of commercial vehicles were available to operators who could obtain a new vehicle licence from the Ministry of War Transport and AEC engines were often fitted to Atkinson, Bristol, Daimler, ERF and Maudslay vehicles.

Below:
At the beginning of the war some uncompleted chassis were finished and allocated to operators who could obtain a new vehicle licence from the Ministry of War Transport. One such delivery was this Mammoth Major 8 to R. Stokes, then running a service benefiting the war effort. Note the offside headlamp mask and the white painted edges to the front wings. The nearside headlamp would not have a bulb fitted, but later in the war the lighting restrictions were relaxed and two masked headlamps were permitted.

Above:
New vehicles being scarce many of the ones due for scrapping were kept in service. This petrol engined Majestic had worked for Truman, Hanbury, Buxton & Co of Burton-on-Trent for over nine years (see page 22) and was due for retirement. However, it was sent to the AEC depot at Nottingham where it was fitted with a reconditioned engine, had body repairs and a major modification and was then ready for a second lease of life.

Left:
The famous Army Matador four-wheel drive gun tractor in its original form. Note the nearside door at the front of the body with the canvas tilt covering the upper part. The cupola on the nearside of the cab roof was used for observation purposes — the observer standing on the passenger seat.

Below left:
Another Matador (Model 0853) fitted with metal 'box' type body for use of the Signal Corps (now Royal Corp of Signals), as a wireless cabin.

Above:
The Matador chassis and cab with flat general service body as used by the RAF.

Below:
The AEC Marshal (Model 854) 6×6 units used by the RAF for refuelling aircraft throughout the sphere of their operations. The tank had a capacity of 2,500gal, and the vehicles were also fitted with a winch.

Above right:
The 4×4 AEC Armoured Car Mk I powered by the 7.7litre engine and equipped with 2pdr gun and co-axially mounted 7.92mm BSA machine gun. The weight of the vehicle was 12ton.

Right:
Another view of the Mk I Armoured Cars fitted with a dummy gun for photographic purposes.

Above left:
The Armoured Car Mk II and Mk III were powered by the 9.6litre oil engine mounted at the rear. The forward compartment was for the driver, while the crew of three were in the centre compartment with the electrically operated turret. The wheelbase was 11ft 4¾in, the overall length was 18ft 5in and the overall width was 8ft 10½in.

Left:
The AEC design for the Flail mine-sweeping tank.

Above:
An experimental Matador with tracked rear drive. Made to a War Department specification it was found to have no better traction than the standard 4×4 Matador in desert sand for which it was intended.

Above right:
The AEC 4×4 Armoured Command Vehicle based on the Matador chassis (7.7litre oil engine) used as a Field HQ.

Right:
The Matador 4×4 with six-pounder gun and armoured protection for the crew. This type of vehicle became famous in the North African campaign and as they were painted yellow to blend with the sandy terrain were known as the 'Yellow Devils'.

Above:
One of the few private commercial vehicles made available in 1942 was the Mammoth Major 8 supplied to William Butler & Co (Bristol) Ltd. The 2,500gal tank was designed for carrying tar or light spirit and was built by Thompson Bros (Bilston) Ltd.

Right:
The last of 9,619 AEC 4×4 Matadors leaving the Southall assembly line at 2.45pm on 5 November 1945, almost five years to the day since it began to produce, in quantity, machines for the Fighting Services. At the wheel is Joan Latham, a wartime worker who had been at Southall since 1941. Behind the appropriately decorated Matador is an AEC Regent double-deck bus chassis included in AECs immediate postwar production programme.

Below right:
When released by the Army many hundreds of Matadors saw service among fairground operators. This one, with flambouyant lettering on its rebuilt bodywork, was at Wanstead Flats Easter Fair in 1975.

5 Postwar 1945-53

When the hostilities were over, the demand for civilian vehicles was almost overwhelming and AEC were not long in getting back to peacetime production, inspite of the fact that many of the government controls were still in existence and were to last for a few years, plus in addition there was a chronic shortage of materials. The government were giving top priority to export orders, yet at the same time they were not aiding the vehicle manufacturers by restricting the length and width of vehicles allowed on the roads of the UK — as well as still maintaining the legal 20mph speed limit for heavies. Thus manufacturers were forced to produce two distinct models — one for the home market and one for export.

The first postwar commercial vehicle off the production lines was the Monarch Mk III 12tonner in the summer of 1945. This was basically the same as the prewar version except that the engine was now a six-cylinder one of 7.7litre capacity, the gear ratios were changed and the rear axle was now fitted with roller bearings instead of the plain ones previously used. At the same time London Transport renewed its contract with AEC for the supply of their buses for another five years.

The last army Matador was driven from the production line on 25 November of the same year (1945) and such was the speed of civilian production that on 4 April 1946 the 1,000th postwar vehicle was produced, but this figure does include both buses and coaches.

Below:
Continuing the prewar design, this Mammoth Major 8 was delivered early in 1947 to a well known firm of general carriers who, unfortunately, lost their identity when they became nationalised a year or so later.

Civilian production was limited to the Monarch and Matador rigid four wheel 12tonners, the latter much as its prewar counterpart but three sizes of tyres could be fitted and it was available with two different wheelbases 14ft 7in or 16ft 7in. The other two vehicles were the Mammoth Major 6 and the Mammoth Major 8, both fitted with the 9.6litre six-cylinder oil engine giving 125bhp.

From 1 January 1948 the production models were renumbered and the prefix 'O' denoting an oil engine was dropped as all vehicles were now fitted for this type of fuel and in fact had virtually been so since 1936.

In April 1948 AEC took over the whole of the share capital of Crossley Motors Ltd of Stockport who had been in business since 1912 and were mainly engaged in the manufacture of buses and coaches. Their demise was swift and Crossley vehicles and their plant were extinct within two years.

In June of the same year AEC acquired the old established (1903) business of Maudslay Motor Co of Coventry, who at that time, were producing the Mogul and Militant four-wheelers; the Mustang twin-steer six-wheeler; the Maharajah a rigid 13ton six-wheeler and the Meritor a rigid 15ton eight-wheeler, plus one coach chassis (Marathon). As all these models were in direct competition with AEC models they were quickly withdrawn, although some were continued until 1951 with an AEC badge, and the others were really badge-engineered AECs.

Following these two acquisitions it was decided that from 1 October 1948 the Associated Equipment Company should change its name to Associated Commercial Vehicles Ltd who would be the holding company for the Group and that AEC Limited would be a subsidiary company dealing with the manufacture and selling. This was purely an administrative move and did

not affect the familiar AEC badge on the radiator. On paper the acquisitions meant that there would be less duplication of competing models, the centralising of resources, and the pooling of experience and design.

ACV, like other manufacturers in 1949/50 were suffering some set-backs for while their order books were full, it comprised many orders for overseas customers who badly wanted vehicles, but who could not pay for them due to currency restrictions in their own country or difficulties with the exchange rates. Meanwhile, the UK customers who could pay for them were not allowed new vehicles due to government restrictions. This, plus the effects of the nationalisation of the Road Haulage industry, and the imposition of Purchase Tax on the basic price of new vehicles, were all to have their effect on the fortunes of AEC and ACV.

In 1949, in response to a demand from some overseas customers, AEC introduced their 11.3litre direct injection overhead valve engine. This new and more powerful unit had many features common to the existing 9.6litre engine having a bore of 130mm by 142mm stroke which developed 150bhp at 1,800rpm.

AEC engines were incorporated into vehicles built by the Canadian Car & Foundry Co Ltd at their plant at Fort William (Canada) where over 3,000 of the Brill buses were produced, plus a large number of trolleybuses for the Montreal Tramways Co fleet.

Two further acquisitions were made in 1949 when the bodybuilding firms of Park Royal Vehicles Ltd and their subsidiary Charles H. Roe of Leeds were taken over. These had little effect on the commercial vehicle manufacture except that at a later date the former company designed and built the new AEC cabs.

At about this time ACV were exporting many vehicles to Spain and the South American countries under the

name ACLO (Associated Company's Lorries and Omnibuses). This name had been registered as far back as 1924 when AEC tried to register their own bar and circle trademark in South America but found that AEG (Allgemeine Elektrixitats Gesellschaft), the German electrical concern had a similar design.

In 1950 it was announced that the Matador II would henceforth be known as the Mandator Mk III (model No 3472/4/5).

Military vehicles were again rolling from the production lines at Southall in 1952 when an order for 6×6 and 6×4 Militants was completed for the Army and other Services.

Above left:
Based on an AEC Regal oil-engined single deck bus chassis this three stall horsebox was built by Vincents of Reading in 1946 for the transport of racehorses belonging to HM King George VI. It was still being used for horses owned by HM Queen Elizabeth II in 1953.

Left:
A 1947 Monarch short wheelbase (12ft 1in) chassis, at that time usually associated with tip lorries. The bodywork and tower is by Eagle Engineering Co. The height of the three section tower when closed is 13ft but fully extended by hydraulic ram from the engine take-off is 22ft. The platform, which can revolve, is 9ft by 4ft.

Right:
Huddersfield Corporation Passenger Transport Department took delivery of two Matador III tower wagons in 1950. The one shown here has the same tower with the same dimensions as the previous illustration.

Above:
An example of the postwar export drive. This difficult-to-recognise Matador semi-trailer unit has full fronted cab similar to motor coaches at that time. The unit carries dairy produce and fish from Denmark to France, Belgium, Switzerland and Czechoslovakia.

Above:
Placed in service in the summer of 1949 this more conventional looking Mammoth Major 6 and two trailers transport 900 sheep in Australia. The double-deck body and trailers were locally manufactured by McGrath of Melbourne. Each trailer is 32ft long and the total length of the complete train is 114ft.

Below:
A Monarch tipper operated by the Road Haulage Executive from their Canterbury (Kent) depot.

Right:
Dropsided body fitted with lattice extensions on a Monarch III which was supplied in 1950 for the transport of market garden produce.

Below right:
A Matador III with dropside body from the same year.

Above and left:
This corrugated high-sided tipping body by Northern Aluminium Co carries 15ton of coal on this Mammoth Major fitted with the 9.6litre engine. The smaller illustration shows the environment in which the lorry works. The tipping gear is manufactured by Pilot Works of Bolton.

Below left:
The angular cab of the Monarch II tractive unit contrasts with the smooth contour of the British Trailer Co semi-trailer van which was supplied to a domestic appliance manufacturer.

Above right:
An ACLO Matador tractor and semi-trailer operated by Transportes Castella which makes two or three weekly trips between Santa Fe and Buenos Aires (351 miles apart) carrying 20ton of chickens and/or fresh eggs.

Right:
A. Pannell of London, NW11, obtained a contract in 1953 for waste disposal from the Lambeth Borough Council. Each of a fleet of eight (seven of which are shown here) AEC Mammoth Majors with moving floor discharge bodies by Glover, Webb & Liversidge can handle 40cu yd of refuse.

Above:
A 4,000gal tank body on a Mammoth Major 8 as delivered to British Road Services in 1954.

Above left:
With Pilot twin underbody tipping gear and steel sided body the normal tail door could be detached and replaced with a scow end. The 1953 Mammoth Major 6 has a wheelbase of 11ft 8in.

Left:
A platform bodied Mammoth Major 6 operated by a Chelmsford Flour Miller passing the Tower of London.

Below:
The Burmese Government operate this tar spraying Mammoth Major IV with cab and 1,500gal tank manufactured by Bonallack.

Above:
This Mandator tractive unit regularly operated for the Great Northern Railway in Ireland with this tanker semi-trailer or with a low loading semi-trailer.

Left:
The bodywork of this van, including the cab and trailer is hardwood framed and aluminium panelled by Gover, Webb and Liversidge. The body, which features a detachable second floor plus a Burtonwood tailboard loader, can carry 150 gas cookers or 2,250 gas meters. The internal length of the van body is 20ft and the trailer 21ft 6in. Both have a height of 7ft 2in and are 6ft 8in wide. The Mandator II chassis has the 9.6litre engine.

Below left:
Fitted to a Mammoth Major 8, the Pilot alloy body carries 24cu yd of coal and is 18ft 8in long by 7ft 2in wide and 5ft high.

Above right:
Basically a commercial model but modified to meet service requirements this 6×4 10ton general service tanker carries 2,500gal of fuel. The tank is divided into five compartments and the pumping arrangements ensure an output of 80gal per minute against a 25ft head and 15ft suction lift. One of the many supplied to the Ministry of Defence in 1954.

Right:
A Mammoth Major tanker operated by Harold Wood & Sons Ltd for Shell Chemical Manufacturing Co which regularly ran between Shell's Stanlow plant and customers at Bromborough, Cheshire, carrying 13ton of liquid sulphur. The tank had steam heating connections for easy discharge of the load.

53

Left:
Silver Roadways obtained this Mammoth Major 8, 15ton platform lorry with 9.6litre engine in 1953 ex-British Road Services, while the twin-steering vehicle came from the same source and had already completed 15 years service when purchased by its new operator.

Below:
Finished in beige and bright red this Mammoth Major 8 with 11.3litre engine can carry the equivalent of six rail wagons full of sheep, or lambs, or 18 fat cows! The SMT triple deck body measures 28ft in length.

Right:
A 6cu yd concrete mixer on a Mammoth Major 6 chassis supplied in 1955.

Below right:
This twin-steer Monarch chassis was often known as 'the Chinese six-wheeler' and seen here with a large capacity van body.

Above:
'Badge engineering'. A Maudslay Monarch twin-steer, which
shows little of any Maudslay ancestry.

Right and below :
Equipped with three-way tipping gear, by Edwards Bros
(Tippers) Ltd of Bolton, this 6×6 Militant is one of the many
supplied to the Ministry of Defence in 1953.

At the end of 1953, AEC announced their new Mercury (Model GM4RA) which was noted for its more modern 'rounded' cab, for up to this time the traditional AEC cab had remained virtually unchanged on all models since the early 1930s. The Mercury was designed to carry an 8ton payload within the legal gross weight of 12ton on its four wheels. When operating with a trailer the gross train weight was 18ton. It was fitted with a choice of the 6.75litre engine given 98bhp at 2,000rpm or the famous 7.7litre engine having 112bhp at 2,000rpm. There was also a choice of three different wheelbases.

Making its debut at the Commercial Motor Show of 1954 was the AEC model 0860 6×6 tractor (later called the Militant) designed for a gross combination weight of 32ton (40ton in countries where the regulations permitted) and a direct successor to the famous Matador. The new chassis was powered by the 11.3litre engine delivering 150bhp. A two-speed auxiliary box transmitted the drive to either the rear bogie or all three axles. Air operated brakes were fitted as standard. Also on view at the Show was a new form of power steering fitted to an AEC Mammoth Major Mk III six-wheel chassis.

In November 1954, Lord Brabazon, a director of ACV, formally opened the new Spares and Service building at Southall which replaced the one lost by enemy bombing in 1940. The new building covered an area of 58,000sq ft plus a two-storey office block of a further 18,000sq ft and cost £250,000.

The 1956 Commercial Motor Show saw the introduction of the new Mercury Mk II (Model 2GM4RA) which was introduced to meet the revised Ministry of Transport regulations which permitted a 14ton gross weight instead of the previous 12ton. The engine was the AVU470, which was the proven 7.7litre engine redesignated. The new vehicle had a heavier frame and front and rear axles plus better brakes. As well as the three wheelbases it could also be obtained as a tractor. At the same show the new Mandator appeared also with the new style cab and this chassis was also available in four different wheelbases with a choice of the 9.6 or 11.3litre engine.

The first AEC off-the-road earth moving vehicle was produced at Southall in 1957 and was the Model 3673, a 6×4 Dumptruck with a capacity of 10cu yd. The machine was to be the fore-runner of many differing Dumptrucks manufactured during the next 10 years.

The change to the new cab or 'wrap-round-front' was completed by the showing of the new Mammoth Major 8 and the new Mandator Mk V tractor at the Commercial Show in September 1958. Other innovations were that the Mercury Mk II could now be fitted with air suspension, while a 4×4 version of the Mercury, to be called a Matador, was announced but it appears that this never went into production. There was also a bonneted version of the Mammoth Major 6 to serve as a tractive unit for the export market. The new Dumptruck was also shown on the stand.

In March 1960 AEC announced their new Marshal medium weight 6×4 model (GM6), which had been developed chiefly for overseas service, for gross weight of 20ton and shared many components common to both the Mercury and the Monarch VI two axle vehicles. The front end of the new vehicle was similar to the Monarch, but the rear had an Eaton-Hendrikson fully articulated double drive bogie.

The industry was surprised to hear in December 1960 that ACV had purchased the whole of the share capital of Transport Equipment (Thornycroft) of Basingstoke. Statements made at the time intimated that the name of Thornycroft would not disappear, but alas within a very short time their normal medium and heavy duty range of trucks and lorries were no longer produced, and even their specialised off-the-road vehicles soon lost their identity.

About this time ACV made financial investments in two new undertakings, one in Central Africa and one in South Africa, linked to an existing organisation J. H Plane whereby vehicles were manufactured mainly from CKD parts. Similar arrangements were made in Belgium with Establissments Spitals and in Holland with NV Auto-Industrie Verheul, the large Netherlands bodybuilder. In 1962 an agreement was also reached with the French Willeme concern who henceforth used AEC engines and became an AEC producer in France using mainly Mandator and Monarch units with their own style cab.

At the end of 1961 the new chassis despatch building was opened at Southall bringing the total covered area at the works to nearly one million sq ft. This building was part of the expanded production facilities as chassis were driven off the assembly line to the new building for road testing and final painting.

In 1962 the new 6×2 Marshal appeared which was the same as the 6×4 version with the exception of the rear axle. It was fitted with a Park Royal plastics cab and used the AV470 engine which could carry a 15ton payload within the legal limit of 20ton gross. The Commercial Motor Show for that year was the debut for the bonneted (normal control) AEC Mogul heavy duty two-axle tractor chassis for the export market. The Mogul was a Maudslay name, but the new model had little affinity to that company. A sister vehicle was the three-axle Majestic which likewise was for the export market. Both were powered by the AV690 200bhp engine.

A few weeks prior to the Commercial Motor Show came news that had a far reaching effect and shocked all sections of the road transport industry when it was learnt in August 1962 that, following secret meetings, the Leyland shareholders had agreed to acquire all the shares of Associated Commercial Vehicles. Followers of the Stock Exchange may have noticed that AEC shares had been falling over a period and that Leyland had been making purchases of such shares. It was felt in many quarters that this was the beginning of the end for AEC — which later proved correct.

Specification for Mercury Mk II (Model GM4RA) forward control 14ton chassis

Engine: AV470 six-cylinder 112mm bore by 130mm stroke, 7.7litre giving 112bhp at 2,000rpm.
Clutch: Single dry plate 14in dia.
Gears: 5-speed synchromesh.
Rear axle: Spiral bevel drive.
Brakes: Air assisted.
Wheels and tyres: 10-20 14 ply (twins on rear). 9-20 (twins on rear) for tractor.
Chassis weight: Average 3.72ton — varies according to wheelbase.
Wheelbase: 11ft 6in, 14ft 6in, 17ft 3in, 8ft 9in
Overall length: 22ft 9in, 26ft 9in
Body space: 13ft 2¾in, 17ft 6½in, 21ft 6½in
Overall width: 7ft 11in
Fuel tank: 36gal

Above:
The first of the 'rounded cabs' in 1953. The AEC Mercury 8ton lorry shown here as an AEC demonstrator.

Left:
Somewhat naturally, the local council supported their home product. An Edbro tipping body of 10¼cu yd capacity is on a Mercury chassis.

Above right:
A Mercury tractor and low loading semi-trailer move a mobile crane in 1956.

Right:
The traditional cab was still fitted to the Mammoth Major in 1955. This tanker by Thompson Bros (Bilston) Ltd has five compartments and can carry 4,000gal of petrol or white spirit, 3,800gal of vaporising oil or 3,300gal of heavy fuel oil. The all metal light alloy cab has sliding doors and was built by Reeve & Kenning Ltd. Overall length of the vehicle is 30ft and the overall height 10ft 6in.

Above:
Another Mercury tractive unit, but with a Dyson semi-trailer fitted with Frigidaire refrigeration equipment for the transport of 100 pig carcasses. Dimensions of the body are 24ft by 7ft 6in by 10ft high.

Left and below left:
The first AEC Dumptruck (Model 3673M) produced in late 1956 also known as Mammoth Major 6 Dumper. Fitted with the 11.3litre engine it had a five-speed gearbox plus a two-speed auxiliary box driving through a $15\frac{1}{4}$in single dry plate clutch. The Edbro tipping gear raised the 10cu yd body to an angle of 70°. Equipped with 15.00×20 22ply tyres, the wheelbase was 12ft $10\frac{1}{2}$in, overall length 23ft 1in and overall width 9ft. The all-steel cab was by Park Royal.

Above right:
Two Mercury special cement carrying tankers, part of a large fleet operated by Clyde Portland Cement Co.

Right:
A Mercury engaged in the transport of grain in bulk with alloy body built by Duramin Engineering Co Ltd. The grain is discharged through two ports at the rear.

Above right and right:
The 1959 Dumptruck (Model HDK4) had an 18cu ft body
(average payload 28ton) powered by the AV1100 turbo charged
six-cylinder engine giving 340bhp. The overall height of the
vehicle is 13ft. The Scottish Land Development Corporation of
Glasgow were sole concessionaires for AEC Dumptrucks.

Below:
The 'rounded cab' was finally fitted to all models in the AEC
range as shown on this Mammoth Major 8 with Bonallack
20cu yd light alloy body and Edbro tipping gear.

Above left and left:
Nearside and offside views of a new (c1959) Mammoth Major tanker, part of a fleet operated by Shell Mex & BP Ltd, in their old livery of red and green.

Below:
British Road Services operated a large fleet of Mandator tractors, the overall length of this articulated unit is 33ft.

Above right:
A later model of the Mandator tractive unit for BRS.

Right:
Channel Transport Services of Australia operate this road train.
The vehicle is a bonneted (export model) Mammoth which is
24ft long and hauls a 32ft long two-axle trailer and a three-axle
trailer of 40ft, thus making a total length of 120ft. The train
carries 60 cattle over long distances for which a 100gal fuel tank
is fitted behind the cab.

Below:
During the 1960s AEC entered the fire appliance field in
association with Merryweather. This Merryweather Marquis is
based on an AEC Mercury with the AV470 engine and five-
speed gearbox. The appliance carries a 100gal first aid tank with
two hose reels of 180ft each and can pump 950gal at 70lbs per
sq in pressure. It is for delivery to Hong Kong Fire Brigade.

Above:
Based on the same chassis and also for Hong Kong this machine is for relaying water and apart from a 45ft light alloy ladder can pump 2,000gal per minute at 100lbs per sq in.

Right:
A Dempster DB30 Dumpmaster Compaction body mounted on a Mammoth Major. The 30cu yd nominal capacity body can handle up to 75cu yd of loose materials by compacting with its 25ton ram. Discharge is by releasing the rear doors and reversing the ram.

Below right:
Seen on the northbound carriageway of the London Colney By-pass this Mammoth Major has a sided body with sheeted roof for ease of loading and unloading via a crane.

Above right:
A Mandator tractive unit with 15ton York tandem axle semi-trailer in operation between the UK, Paris and Germany.

Right:
One of 18 — 15ton Dumptrucks operated by the South African Railways and Harbours. Built in South Africa, with the AV690 engine, the bodies are by Steel Construction Co of Johannesburg. Pilot twin ram tipping gear is employed.

Below:
A 690 Dumptruck for a 15ton payload (heaped is 12cu yd) in typical operating terrain.

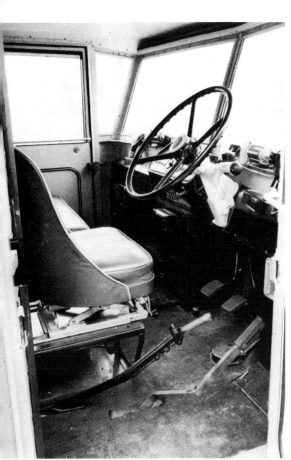

Left:
The driving cab of the 690 Dumptruck which is similar to the 1100 type.

Below:
A Mercury tipper for 12-14ton gross weight operation. Two wheelbases were available, this one being the shorter type.

Bottom:
In the new livery of white, yellow and grey this Mandator tractor with the AV690 engine and six-speed gearbox has a frameless semi-trailer tank body for 3,700gal by the Steel Barrel Co. The diameter of the tank is 5ft 6in and the length 27ft. Carrimore running gear forms the basis of the tanker

Left:
Easy entry into the cab of a Mandator tractive unit.

Below:
The Marshal 6×4 chassis proved popular for cement mixers as shown here in 1962 with a 6cu yd example.

Far right top:
With a moulded plastics cab by Road Transport Services and expanded metal dropsides this Mammoth Major 8 is well equipped for the haulage of bricks.

Right:
Loading 16ton of crushed phosphate rock by remote control into a Mammoth Major.

Far right centre:
Unloading the same material from the vehicle by discharging into an underground silo.

Below right:
A skip body mounted on a Mammoth Major with a wheelbase of 14ft 8in. Operated by Harold Wood & Son Ltd the vehicle has a payload of $11\frac{3}{4}$ton of scrap metal.

Above:
This Mammoth Major was a 1963 delivery to Shell Mex & BP Gases Ltd. The Park Royal plastics cab is fitted to the chassis which has a 4,500gal tank by F. A. Harvey & Co for the conveyance of liquid butane.

Left:
An interesting articulated unit comprising a Mammoth Major 8 and tandem bogies or dollies built from Mammoth Major parts. Operated by Heavy Abnormal Transport Services Ltd it is carrying 20ton loads of 4ft long steel pipes from Stockton-on-Tees to Canvey Island and capable of cruising on Motorways at 55mph.

Below left:
An unusual but attractive look for the front end of a Mandator tractor unit fitted with a Belgium made Bollekens all-steel sleeper cab in 1964.

Above and left:
Built on a Mercury chassis this Merryweather 100ft turntable ladder was supplied to the London Fire Brigade in 1964. The smaller illustration shows the hydraulic jacks extended for rigidity while the ladder operator's controls and seat can be seen on the nearside rear.

Below left:
A Mammoth Major 6 employed as the prime mover of a mobile car crushing plant. The total length of the outfit is 40ft and the weight nearly 50ton.

Above:
An example of badge engineering. An AEC Mustang twin-steering chassis with stainless steel tank body operated by Watneys Brewery. We presume that the water only goes on the outside of the tank!

Left:
The Marshal (Model GM6R) introduced in 1960 mainly for export with Eaton rear axles, Hendrikson spring suspension and air brakes.

Below left:
An AEC Mogul tractor unit for export only.

Above right:
An export Mammoth Major 8 as a tractive unit with a tandem axle semi-trailer which has a payload of 19½ton operated by Clan Transport of Salisbury, Southern Rhodesia.

Right:
The International Ferrymasters concern operates this Mandator 192bhp tractor unit, seen here en route to Finland.

7 The Final Years 1964–1979

The first outward change with the Leyland merger (or should it be take-over) was apparent at the 1964 Commercial Motor Show when the AEC stand featured the Leyland Ergomatic cab on their models. While the AEC 'rounded cab' had been acclaimed as a great advance over their original cabs, nevertheless they were not so well insulated against noise and there was less leg room compared to the latest offerings from competitors. Apart from greater driver comfort the new Ergomatic cab featured a torsion bar tilt mechanism that permits one hand tilting to a 55° angle, plus double skin construction giving good insulation and sound proofing. In addition heater and demister controls were fitted as standard and the one piece windscreen (6ft 3in wide by 2ft 5in deep) gives good visibility aided by nearside and offside rear-view mirrors mounted on brackets.

The vehicles shown on the stand represented the range at that time and were the Mercury 16ton gross rigid 4×2, and a short wheelbase tractor version for 24ton gross; the Marshal 6×4 for 22ton gross; the Mandator 4×2 tractor for 32ton gross; and the Mammoth Major 6 and Mammoth Major 8. The latter available in two wheelbases (14ft 5½in or 17ft 2in).

A new series of engines was also announced based on the earlier types but with dry liners, the designation number approximating to the cubic capacity — AV471 (469cc) 7.6litre replacing AV470; AV505 is 8.1litre; AV691 is 11.3litre and AV760 is 12.4litre.

The twin-steer Mammoth Minor tractor unit (Model TG6RF) was announced in 1965. This vehicle was intended for a 32gross combined weight combination having a wheelbase of 12ft 2½in and overall length of 19ft 6in. It could be supplied with either the AV691

205bhp engine or the AV760 226bhp engine and was fitted with a six-speed, overdrive top, gearbox.

There were no major changes in the next few years, only some differing options of engines and/or transmission systems, and the AEC production and sales were on the downward trend, having lost several contracts and a rapidly declining export market.

In 1968 AEC announced their new 800 series V8 engine which apart from sitting lower in the chassis had greatly increased power to weight ratio and fuel economy. The company were pinning great hopes on the new engine which with cylinders having a bore of 130mm and stroke of 114mm the 12.1litre unit developed 247bhp at 2,600rpm. It was first fitted to a Mandator tractor (Model VTG4R) for 32ton gross and in September was shown at the Commercial Motor Show at Earls Court in a Mammoth Major 6 tractive unit (Model 2VTG6) for 44ton gross weight with three-axle semi-trailer.

Right:
The large Dumptrucks were still being manufactured in the mid-60s and this unusual view shows the 10cu yd type fitted with Edbro tipping gear.

Below:
The new look AEC. The Leyland Ergomatic cab fitted to an AEC Mercury tractor with a British Trailer Company semi-trailer designed for refrigerated transport. The AV505 engine which develops 165bhp is used in the tractive unit.

Unfortunately, the new engine was not a success and for the first time an AEC engine gave considerable trouble. It is thought that insufficient development and testing was due to financial shortages, as budgeted expenditure was taken for the British Leyland car plant, plus the possibility of the sales side of British Leyland urging its availability, all counted towards its failure. The damage to the AEC prestige was incalculable and from that time onwards AEC declined rapidly.

During 1968 the familiar AEC badge and triangle began to disappear from the front of their vehicles to be replaced by the British Leyland roundel set in a square, although the initials AEC and the name of the model still appeared above the front bumper.

By 1974 the name AEC had virtually disappeared on new commercial vehicles and the Southall factory was producing the Leyland Marathon, the then, top weight vehicle in their range.

Bus production continued for a little over a year, but the failure of two AEC types and with Leyland concentrating on their single-deck National and a dwindling bus industry generally, it was announced at the end of 1978 that the Southall works would close. The decline had started soon after the Leyland take-over and although slowly at first it had gathered momentum as the years passed. It is easy to be wise after an event, but possibly if different decisions had been made in the 1960s, AEC would still be with us today.

The Southall Works finally closed down on 25 May 1979.

Specification for Mammoth Minor Type TG6RF forward control 32ton tractor
Engine: AV760 six-cylinder 136mm bore by 142mm stroke 12.47litre giving 226bhp at 2,200rpm.
Clutch: Single 17in dia dry plate, air assisted.
Gears: Six-speed constant mesh with overdrive top.
Rear axle: Double reduction.
Brakes: Air operated.
Wheels and tyres: 4.20 (twins on rear).
Wheelbase: 12ft 2½in.
Overall length: 19ft 6in.
Overall width: 7ft 11½in

Specification for Mandator (Type VTG4) normal control 32ton tractor
Engine: V8, 130mm bore by 114mm stroke giving 247bhp at 2,600rpm.
Clutch: 17¾in fluid.
Gears: Ten-speed semi automatic transmission using five-speed direct acting epicyclic main gearbox with splitter section. Air operated.
Rear axle: Double reduction spiral bevel drive fully floating.
Brakes: Air operated footbrake on all wheels.
Wheels and tyres: 10.00-20 (Twins on rear).
Chassis weight: 5ton 2qr.
Wheelbase: 9ft 6in.
Overall length: 16ft 9½in.
Overall width: 7ft 11½in.
Height to top of cab: 8ft 6½in.
Fuel: 75gal tank.

Above:
An AEC Mogul (export model) tractor fitted with 200bhp engine hauls a Boden semi-trailer with open top across most parts of Europe.

Left:
The Ergomatic cab in the tilted position showing the accessibility of the engine and components.

Above right:
An AEC Marquis Fire Appliance supplied to the City of Leicester Fire Brigade, which neatly incorporates the Ergomatic cab front, but without any identification badge.

Right:
Rear three-quarter view of the above appliance. Note the stays for holding the escape ladder.

Above left:
Mandator tractor unit with a Bonallack frameless light alloy tanker semi-trailer for carrying cement in bulk, which is discharged by air pressure. The gross weight of the outfit is 28ton.

Left:
The new Mammoth Minor twin-steer tractor unit for 32ton gross train weight seen here at its debut at the Scottish Motor Show, Kelvin Hall, Glasgow in 1965.

Above:
A Monarch rigid 4×2 equipped with twin 40gal fuel tanks and power assisted steering. The all-alloy refrigerated body was built by Silverdale Motor Bodies of Birmingham and is 21ft long with a payload capacity of 9ton. The vehicle, specially built for export, operated from Switzerland to all parts of Europe and the Mediterranean carrying supplies for the American Armed Forces.

Below:
Another view of the Mammoth Minor tractor unit fitted with the AEC AV760 engine producing 226bhp at 2,200rpm.

Above:
A Marshal tipper operated by J. W. Jackson & Son of West Rasen, Lincs.

Below:
A Mammoth Minor tractor and flat bed semi-trailer carrying 14 totebins of 110cu ft capacity each holding Polymer chips for making Bri-nylon. The vehicle operated on a round the clock basis between Wilton and ICI factories at Gloucester, Pontypool and Doncaster.

Above right:
British Road Services in 1966 took delivery of two Marshal rig six vehicles each having a gross weight of 22ton.

Right:
A 1969 Mercury with AV505 engine of 161bhp. The steel side body has its own crane for loading and off-loading.

Left:
A 1966 Mandator tractor with AV691 220bhp engine hauling TIR trailers between customers' premises and the European ferry centres. The vehicle is finished in the orange and white livery of Ferrymasters.

Below:
A 1967 Mammoth Major 6 short wheelbase unit with a Dyson 40-45ton machinery low loading semi-trailer, the flat deck of which is 22ft long.

Bottom:
Exported to Australia in 1967 is this Mammoth Major 8 prime mover which hauls a semi-trailer of 8,290gal capacity and a gross train weight of 40ton. The overall length of the outfit is 47

Right:
This Mandator tractor unit operates at 32ton GCW having a maximum payload of 22ton 2cwt. The 40ft York semi-trailer carries imported sections of pipes for North Sea gas.

Below right:
One of the biggest bulk refuse tippers operating in Great Britain in 1967. The Mammoth Major 6 hauls a semi-trailer with a payload of 17ton and a capacity of 65cu yd. The unit operated on a GLC contract by Richard Biffa Ltd with body and tipping gear by Telehoist.

Above:
This Mercury tractor and semi-trailer is being loaded with a 40ft long 58-seat cruise launch for the liner *Queen Elizabeth II*. The loading is being undertaken by the makers, Watercraft of East Molesey for transport to the Boat Show at Earls Court in 1968 before final delivery to the customer at Southampton.

Right:
An opening roof semi-trailer with curtain sides for a 22ton payload coupled to a Mandator tractor.

Above:
One of the three Mammoth Major (Model TG6RB) 11ft 6in wheelbase tippers supplied to the National Coal Board. The 10cu yd all-steel dumper type body, which is 8in wider at the rear than the front, was built by Edbro Ltd of Bolton.

Right:
Prior to the new 800 series V8 engine being introduced it was tested in differing countries. Here it is fitted into a Vanaja bonneted vehicle operating in near arctic conditions in Finland in the winter of 1967/68.

Above:
Another V8 engine prior to the launch was fitted to this Mandator operating in Australia with Freight Transfer Pty Ltd.

Below:
The new V8 engine was introduced in May 1968 and shown here fitted into a Mandator tractor chassis with ten-speed semi-automatic transmission. The low height of the engine can be clearly seen together with a complexity of pipes and wiring, etc.

Right:
Diagram of the V8 Mandator (Model VTG4R) tractor chassis. The dimensions are — A, 9ft 6in; B, 16ft 9½in; C, 11ft 3in; D, 8ft 3in; E, 3ft; G, 4ft 3½in.

Below right:
Close-up view of the Mandator V8 tractor chassis for 32ton gross weight (in UK) with 'Thru-way' Ergomatic cab and ten-speed semi-automatic transmission.

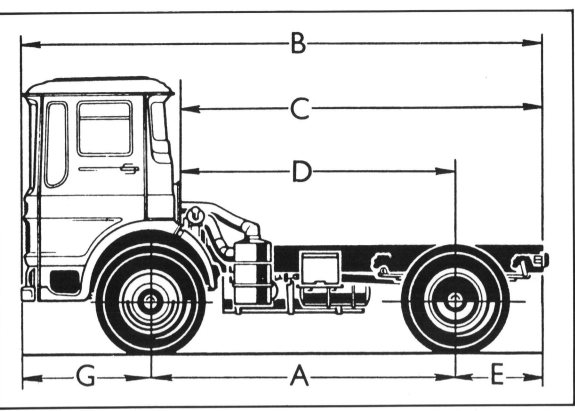

Right:
An interior view of the new V8 Mandator tractor cab. The lower engine permits a three-seater cab with an unobstructive floor space which AEC called the 'Thru-way' cab.

Below:
A Mandator V8 tractor and semi-trailer operated by Ferrymasters on their European services.

Left:
Full frontal! A V8 Mandator chassis for 32ton gross train weight. Note the British Leyland badge has replaced the traditional AEC blue triangle.

Below:
A Mammoth Major 6 — V engine 6×4 prime mover for 56ton gross carrying weight. This model (2VTG6) was originally intended for export only.

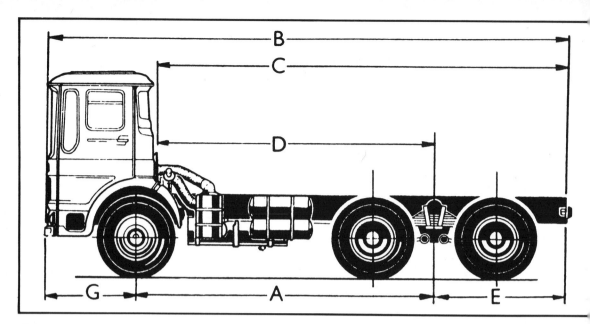

Above:

Diagram of the Mammoth Major 6 — V8 (Model 2VTG6). Three different wheelbases were available and the dimensions are as follows:

A	B	C	D	E	G
11ft 6in	21ft 0½in	15ft 11in	10ft 8in	5ft 3in	4ft 3½in
13ft	24ft 5½in	19ft 4in	12ft 2in	7ft 2in	4ft 3½in
16ft 2in	30ft 1½in	25ft	15ft 4in	9ft 8in	4ft 3½in

Below:

The Marshal 6×4 chassis for 24ton gross vehicle weight and fitted with the AV505 engine developing 165bhp.

Right:

Arduous duties being performed by a 1973 built Mammoth Major 8 tipping lorry for 30ton gross vehicle weight. It is fitted with the AV760 255bhp engine.

Below right:

One of the places where the last AECs will be giving a useful service — the fairground.

8 Service Vehicles

AEC, in common with other manufacturers of heavy vehicles, required small trucks and vans for the delivery of spare parts, service equipment and etc. It was uneconomical to use the heavy vehicles of their own manufacture, thus they used a variety of makes, a few of which are depicted here.

Left:
...ne of the 1939 Austin 2/3ton dropside lorries which were used ... Southall during the war.

Above:
Although a 1937/8 design the Morris Commercial model CV11/40 was used by the Nottingham Depot and Service Department in 1945.

...elow left:
... mid-1930s Morris Commercial dropside lorry photographed ...n the Southall site with the GWR main line in the background.

Below:
The Bradford Depot used this Commer 30cwt van of 1938 vintage in 1946, photographed at the Southall Works.

Above:
A company owned Matador used at the Coventry Depot for towing and salvage work. The close connection with Maudslay is noted by their name on the radiator.

Left:
One of the many main AEC distributors, C.V. (Sales & Repairs) Ltd of Basildon built and operated this Mammoth Major 6 (11ft 9in wheelbase) fitted with the AV691 engine, as a recovery vehicle. It was capable of towing 56ton loads and could make a suspended recovery of 24ton. Complete weight of the vehicle is 10ton 11qwt.

Below:
A 1939 Regal single-deck bus chassis was for many years used as a mobile test bed for new engines, transmissions and rear axles. The saloon behind the half cab was for examiners, inspectors and/or engineers, while the low sided platform at the rear could be loaded with weights to simulate a full load.

List of AEC Commercial Vehicle Models

Years	Model	Description
910-1920	B	Mainly troop carriers. 3½-4ton
916-1921	Y	3/4ton N/C (uprated to 5ton). Later known as 501 type
916-1917	—	Russian B. 2ton N/C (B type shipped CKD to Russia)
923-1924	201-6	2ton N/C
923-1924	701	Experimental six-wheel tractor for artic use
925-1932	506	Granville 4-5ton N/C (few built as psvs)
925-1929	507	Ramillies. 6ton F/C
926-1930	508	4/5ton swb F/C. Development of 506 used as artic or tipper
927-1931	418	3½ton N/C (also ADC)
927-1930	509	6ton F/C (only few produced)
928-1930	428	4ton F/C
930-1937	640	Mercury 4ton N/C
930-1937	641	Monarch 4ton F/C
931-1936	666	Majestic. 6ton N/C
931-1935	667	Mammoth 7/8ton F/C
931-1939	668	Mammoth Major F/C six wheel
931-1941	644	Marshal (MOS) F/C six-wheel
931-1935	645	Matador 6ton F/C
931-1935	669	Mandator F/C
931-1932	672	Mandator N/C
933	643	Mercury F/C
933-1935	647	Monarch 7½ton F/C
933-1935	648	Monarch
933-1937	671	Marshal six-wheel
933-1937	673	Marshal six-wheel
934-1935	646	Mandator 6ton N/C (Export)
933-1935	851	Tractor 8×8. Developed from FWD parts
934-1935	680	Mammoth Major 8
934-1940	344	Monarch Mk I 7/8ton F/C
935-1940	244	Monarch Mk II 7/8ton N/C
935-1947	346	Mandator Mk II 7½ton F/C
935-1940	246	Matador Mk II N/C
935-1948	366	Mammoth Major 6 13½ton F/C
935-1948	386	Mammoth Major 8 15ton F/C
936-1938	OS6	
936-1937	OS10	
937-1941	366	Mammoth Minor lhd
939-1945	853	Matador 10ton F/C 4×4 gun tractor
940-1944	854	Marshal F/C 6×6
942	855	Armoured Car Mk I WD
943-1944	856	Armoured Car Mk II and Mk III
944-1945	857	Armoured Command vehicle 6×6
1948	858	Armoured Command vehicle 6×6
1945-1947	346S	Monarch six-cylinder engine
1947-1956	3451	Monarch Mk III
1947-1949	3471	Matador Mk III
1947-1948	2481	Export N/C model
1948-1957	2482/3	Export N/C model
1948-1960	3871/2/3	Mammoth Major 8 Mk II F/C
1948-1961	3881/2	Mammoth Major 8 Mk III F/C
1948-1960	2671	Mammoth Major 6 Mk III N/C Export
1948-1960	3671/2/3	Mammoth Major 6 Mk III F/C
1949-1962	2681	Mammoth Major 6 Mk III N/C Export
1949-1962	3681/2/3	Mammoth Major 6 Mk III F/C
1950-1961	2472/3	Mandator N/C Export
1950-1961	3472/4/5	Mandator Mk III F/C Export tractor unit
1950-1962	3481/2/3/4	Mandator Mk III F/C Export
1950-1956	3521	Majestic F/C
1951-1957	3531	Majestic F/C
1952-1960	0859	Militant 6×4 F/C (for Army)
1952-1962	0860	Militant 6×6 F/C (for Army)
1952-1961	0880	Militant 6×6 F/C (for Army)
1953-1965	GM4RA	Mercury Mk I & Mk II F/C
1955-1966	GM4LA	Monarch Mk V & Mk VI (Export version of Mercury)
1956-1962	2431	Mammoth Mk III N/C Export
1956-1962	2621	Mammoth Major 6 Mk III Export
1956-1962	2631/2	Mammoth Major 6 Mk III N/C Export
1956-1961	GM6RH	Mustang F/C Export six-wheel
1958-1963	3673M	Dumptruck F/C 6×4 10cu yd
1958-1966	G4RA	Mandator Mk V F/C Tractor
1959-1964	G6RA	Mammoth Major 6 Mk V F/C
1959-1964	G8RA	Mammoth Major 8 Mk V F/C
1959-1966	GB4R	Mogul N/C Export
1959-1968	GB6R	Majestic N/C Export 6×2
1959-1962	HDK4LA	Dumptruck 690
1960-1966	GM6L	Marshal F/C six-wheel
1960-1966	GM6L	Marshal F/C six-wheel
1961-1965	HG6RAB	Super Mammoth Heavy-duty N/C Export
1961-1962	DK6RAB	Dumptruck N/C 10cu yd
1961-1963	DK4RA	Dumptruck N/C 15cu yd
1963-1966	G6LA	Mammoth Major 6 F/C Export
1963-1966	G4LA	Mandator Mk V F/C Export
1964	HDK4	Dumptruck 1100 N/C 27cu yd
1964-1975	TG4R	Mandator F/C Tractor

1964-1976	TGM4R	Mercury F/C
1964-1976	TGM6R	Marshal F/C 6×4
1964-1978	TG6R	Mammoth Major 6 F/C
1964-1978	TGM8R	Mammoth Major 8 F/C
1964	BDK6	Dumptruck 690 N/C (later became Scammell LD55)
1965-1967	TG6RF	Mammoth Minor F/C 6×2 Twin Steer tractor
1968-1970	VTG4R	Mandator V8 F/C Tractor
1967-1968	TGM8R	Marshal F/C 8×4 rigid
1968	2VTG6	Mammoth Major 6 V8 engine F/C prototype

NOTES: Quantity production often did not start until the year following the date of introduction.

Most models had diesel engines fitted from the mid-1930s, but the model number had an 'O' prefix until 1946.

The model numbers introduced from 1956 were coded. Thus TGM4R means it is a Tractor, goods, four-wheel drive, right hand drive.

H after the model number means a double-drive rear axle (H meaning Hardy?).

R after model number means right hand drive, similarly L for left hand drive.

N/C means normal control — ie bonneted or engine in front of cab.

F/C means forward control — no bonnet and cab is over engine.

MOS=Ministry of Supply.
WD=War Department.
swb=short wheelbase.
ADC=Associated Daimler.